Paul McCartney & Wings:

The Story of a Classic Album

SERIES *MILESTONES*

Paul McCartney & Wings:
Band on the Run

The Story of a Classic Album

Luca Perasi

LILY PUBLISHING

BOOKS THAT ROCK!

Published by:

L.I.L.Y. Publishing
Via Tirso, 8
20141 Milan

e-mail: info@lily-publishing.com
Facebook: https://www.facebook.com/paulmccartneymusicisideas
Twitter: https://twitter.com/LucaPerasi
Website: https://www.mccartney-musicisideas.it/

First edition: April 2024
Curator and inner layout: Steve Lambley
Cover project: Steve Lambley

ISBN: 979-12-81758-02-5

10 9 8 7 6 5 4 3 2 1

This book is dedicated to the memory of my dear father
Silvano Perasi (8 April 1944 – 1 November 2022)

and
Tony Clark (2 April 1946 – 27 February 2024)

— TABLE OF CONTENTS —

— INTRODUCTION —

*B*and *on the Run* is undoubtedly the most popular and commercially successful of Paul McCartney's post-Beatles albums. The evidence of this is, among other things, the several re-issues of the record, including CD re-issues, box sets and Deluxe editions that followed one another over the decades.

Hailed since its release in December 1973 as an exceptional accomplishment (and one that allows the critics – who up to that moment, whether rightly or wrongly, had been disappointed by McCartney's offerings, judging them bizarre, disjointed or only sporadically good – to breathe a sigh of relief), *Band on the Run* soon gains a place of honour as a quintessential example of its creator's pop art. Furthermore, it has often been set as a touchstone for his subsequent productions, thus creating, to some extent, a degree of embarrassment. For decades, any critic who wanted to positively assess a new record by Paul McCartney would simply label it as "his best work since *Band on the Run*".

Thus, from that moment to this, the album has enjoyed eternal youth. It's outlived all the fashions of the decades, even "surviving" McCartney's worst moments among critics and audience, as was the case for quite some time in the Eighties. And so, for its influence on popular culture, *Band on the Run* still remains the only McCartney solo production that stands comparison – albeit relatively distantly – with the output of The Beatles.

The reason is easily explained: the path that leads to its release follows the path of those adventures in which the hero (McCartney, in our case) overcomes a series of obstacles: thus, he improvises, he adapts himself and resolves the situation. The hero has also been the narrator over the decades, and this has added further charm to a story that is already incredible.

The facts are widely known in general terms: from the desertion of two Wings members prior to their departure for the album recordings, to the tribulations for Paul, Linda, Denny Laine and engineer Geoff Emerick during their stay in Lagos, Nigeria. Here, McCartney records in extremely difficult conditions, with the EMI studio lacking sound booths and having a recording console where only four tracks can be listened to simultaneously; he faces a major misunderstanding with activist Fela Ransome-Kuti and the local musical/media environment, who accuse him of artistic "colonialism"; he has to use all of his diplomatic skills with ex-Cream drummer Cream Ginger Baker for not using his recording studios, this having been vetoed by EMI; he's robbed of his tapes (the actual content of which is still debated) at knifepoint; he collapses in the studio from a bronchial spasm which prompts fears for his life. Not even the trips between Great Britain and Nigeria go smoothly: on the way there, the pilots struggle to find the landing strip, covered in the mists of the African jungle, while the flight back arrives in Gatwick with a good ten-hour delay.

Even in London, a certain dose of misfortune seems to plague the record. At some point during the sessions, they notice oxide on the tapes, and they need to quickly make a transfer copy of them to avoid losing the recordings. The mixing has to be done in a hurry, before Emerick is dragged away by the producers of another project he was in charge of and that was looming inexorably.

So, is it true, as Mark Lewisohn's sleeve notes say in the 25th Anniversary Edition of the album (1999), that "*Band on the Run* is the proof that art can triumph over adversity"? It's a fascinating view, certainly true, although one that McCartney has fully never endorsed.

Nevertheless, even without wanting to see the hand of fate in the success of this record, it's undeniable that the adventures that have been necessary for its completion speak of something extraordinary, even ignoring the myths that need to be debunked, at least in part. In these terms, it's perhaps the one and only McCartney "rock" record; an album that encompasses the deeds of a hero who rides the stormy seas of events and who manages to save himself, and finally triumphing, notwithstanding all the predictions. A record that brings with it the signs of an incredible story, one that is almost fictional.

Band on the Run arguably represents a watershed within McCartney's post-Beatles career. The exuberance of the songs, the crafting of the arrangements, a certain common thread within the lyrics, which explore the subject of freedom almost creating a concept album, make it a milestone of Seventies rock.

And to think that, when the album appears at the end of 1973, the year has produced some of the best records in musical history, marked by unforgettable classics: from David Bowie's "*Ziggy Stardust* goes to America" follow-up *Aladdin Sane*, to the luxurious Medieval-like fairy tales and rock crossover of Genesis' *Selling England by the Pound*; from Elton John's epic *Goodbye Yellow Brick Road* to Mike Oldfield's symphonic *Tubular Bells*; from the tragic struggles of Lou Reed's *Berlin* to Stevie Wonder's container of sex, drugs, religion, political corruption, *Innervisions*, to name but a few.

This volume offers the chance to retrace a gallery of circumstances, locations, pieces of art and characters somewhat linked to *Band on the Run* and to its creation, that make the album an anthology of cross-pollination between music and other arts, with a special consideration for its visual and filmic aspects.

There's Dustin Hoffman who challenges Paul to write a song about the last words said by Picasso before dying; McCartney would make it a sort of cubist portrayal more than a real song, "Picasso's Last Words", with Dylan in a corner of his mind. There's a puppy, whose name inspires "Jet", the single that will change the commercial fate of the album and where we can glimpse an affectionate nod towards David Bowie. There's the renowned heiress Gloria Vanderbilt, whose name Paul metamorphoses into "Mrs. Vandebilt", making her symbolic of a jet-set from which is better to keep away. In the same song, there are also echoes of the comedy of both Charlie Chester and Laurel and Hardy, of whom Paul has been an admirer since way back.

There's the tribute – deliberate or not, it seems that we'll never know – to the "short echo" used by Lennon in many of his songs of the early Seventies in "Let Me Roll It". There's the famous Marrakesh resort, La Mamounia, which some-how gives its name to "Mamunia", and there are Orwellian echoes, at least in the title, of "Nineteen Hundred and Eighty-Five".

There are the anonymous fugitives of the title track "Band on the Run", who try to escape from a prison, symbolic of a certain state of being "persecuted by the law", something that several rock personalities suffer due to their habit of soft drug consumption; Paul himself pays the price for it when he's arrested in August 1972.

Moreover, the subject of the prisoners on the run, so well depicted in the iconic cover photo – which gathers a handful of celebrities, including actors, politicians and various showbusiness personalities – finds a resounding equiva-lent in the movie *Papillon* (in which one of the two main characters is, irony of fate, Dustin Hoffman), first shown in theatres on the same month as the release of *Band on the Run* and which, to some extent, helps to reinforce its impact on the audience.

This book includes in-depth analyses of various aspects of the record. There are lists, albeit some partial, of the equipment used during the sessions, from the recording console in Lagos to the models of the instruments played by Paul, Linda and Denny: a little illustrated gallery that will please the palate of vintage instrument lovers.

In addition, it's been considered useful to delve into some aspects related to the structure of the songs and their instrumental parts, with a focus on one of the cornerstones around which McCartney has built his narrative of the exceptional nature of *Band on the Run*: his drum parts.

This is a very interesting example not only for McCartney's fans but also for anyone with a passion for recorded music in general: Paul conceives his contri-bution on the instrument in very simple manner, knowing full well that he can't compete with rock's bona fide drummers, and puts in place a series of ideas and "tricks" that again confirm his creativity and skill in finding handcrafted solutions capable of serving him in a suitable manner, leading him to a successful result.

Paul takes as a model Stevie Wonder – who would often play drums on his records, and whose skills on the instrument McCartney himself would see with his own eyes eight years later, when Wonder guests on the album *Tug of War* – but when he finds himself behind the drum kit, he wisely decides not to overdo it, conscious of his technical limitations. Rather than worrying about it, he makes the most out of what he can do, not being afraid to ask for help when needed.

There are few examples in pop-rock music as illuminating as this which confirm without doubt the dominance of inventiveness over technical skills.

The book then focuses on one of the key episodes that conspired to create the myth of *Band on the Run* – the famous (or infamous) robbery of the tapes, the cornerstone of the whole affair. Shaped by McCartney over the course of the decades through a narration that became progressively more detailed, this episode is reconstructed through the statements made by Paul in various interviews, highlighting its contradictions, incongruencies and lapses.

All these statements prove the power of storytelling for the benefit of the media, constructing fascinating anecdotes: McCartney is aware that rock nourishes these kinds of tales, filled with mystery, and took advantage of his skill as a narrator and entertainer to fine-tune one of the most surprising re-enactments that surround rock music masterpieces, on the border between true and plausible, between real and fantastic. I thought it was worth delving into this story, whose partial inconsistencies I had first highlighted in 2016 in my Italian book *I Beatles dopo i Beatles* (*The Beatles after The Beatles*) and also included in the subsequent *Paul McCartney: Music Is Ideas. The Stories Behind the Songs (Vol. 1) 1970–1989* in 2023. Recent research included in the book *The McCartney Legacy. Volume 1: 1969–73* by Allan Kozinn and Adrian Sinclair has proved that this was the right path to take to better understand the events. I have relied on the same book not only for the flow of events but also for recording dates and the instruments attributed to the musicians on a track-by-track basis, something that was known only partially or not so precisely before.

Last but not least, the book contains an exclusive interview – which I conducted back in 2014 and which has remained on the shelf – with engineer Pete Swettenham, who assisted Geoff Emerick during the sessions for the album held at AIR Studios in London. It's an important account, not only because Swettenham is one of the few people who witnessed the recordings who is still alive, but also because his recollections contribute to better clarification of what really happened in the studio when the tapes were oxidising and about the possible related responsibilities. In his autobiography, Emerick ascribes a certain amount of negligence to his assistant, but Swettenham very clearly sheds light once for all on that event and, it has to be said, in a very chivalrous manner.

Band on the Run is also case history in marketing, not only related to the music business. The story of its commercial success is proof that the quality of a product can be given more value by means of promotional strategy planned with care and in detail. Art, if it's of value, has to sell, and not be ashamed of its success. This is the cornerstone of the unparalleled popularity of McCartney (and of The Beatles), that allowed them over the decades to reach sales without comparison in the music business.

It's worth noting in this case that the sequence of events related to the commercial success of *Band on the Run* – concerning both McCartney and the other characters involved – relies on an almost "natural" juxtaposition between the artist, who defends the integrity of his own product, and the marketing machinery of the record company, embodied by promoters hungry for sales and returns, and who grab every opportunity that allows them to "work" the LP.

It's Al Coury, a promoter at Capitol, who pressures McCartney into including the single "Helen Wheels", released on about one month before the album, on the US edition of *Band on the Run*, managing to get Paul's approval, albeit through gritted teeth. And it's Coury again who convinces Paul of the need to extract singles from the album, to increase its popularity and exposure. McCartney, by his own admission, didn't think about this.

It could be just role play, although if so, it is effectively performed; what counts is that the plan set up to push sales of *Band on the Run* by the marketing professionals (among which we can also arguably include McCartney himself) is one of the cleverest ever devised.

Capitol builds its marketing plan on choices that respond to the market itself (Coury chooses "Jet" as a single when he starts receiving increasingly insistent requests from radio stations), on Coury's simple flair or based on the quality of the material, but always modelled with an eye to being as commercial as possible: "Band on the Run", a three-part song that could disorientate listeners and so find difficulty in being aired, is adapted to the 7" single format through an edit that McCartney himself openly praises.

In its simplicity, made by almost casual juxtapositions and by references to the subject of freedom, *Band on the Run* is intelligently constructed. The album has a certain cinematographic quality, something that is dear to McCartney: a narrative thread, the use of contrasts – both within the same song, as for "Band on the Run" and in the case of the track sequence, organised by playing on the variety of tones and atmospheres – a recurring character (Sailor Sam, who is mentioned both in the title track and in "Helen Wheels", although this internal hint can be caught only on the US edition of the record), an opening and an ending that captures the attention, as in every spectacular movie worthy of its name. Because *Band on the Run* is, in its own way, an epic achievement.

At the time of its release, critics agreed about the qualities of *Band on the Run*, maybe even to a somewhat greater extent than it merited. The record's main quality is cohesion: excellent pop songs and musical ideas combined with inspired lyrics – both simple and poetic. Powerful and filled with fictional characters and themes, still to this day *Band on the Run* remains key when telling the story of pop music in the Seventies. And the same goes for its creator.

Luca Perasi

Thanks to

Steve Lambley, Franco Zanetti, Adrian Sinclair, Edward Eikelenboom, Chip Madinger. Laura for the support. Thanks to my family.

—1—
WE'VE HEARD OF THE BEATLES, BUT WE'RE HERE BECAUSE WE'RE WINGS FANS

t's 19 March 1973, and Wings are getting back performing in the UK for the first time since their 1972 *University Tour*, a semi-clandestine matter, with surprise performances held in the ballrooms of the colleges. Similarly, on this occasion, the show is unannounced, and in an intimate environment. The chosen location is the Hard Rock Café, the historic venue just off Park Lane, between Buckingham Palace and Hyde Park. It's a benefit concert, with a mere 200 people in attendance, entrance is £5, three times the price of an average concert.

The five-piece band – consisting of Paul and Linda McCartney, Denny Laine, Henry McCullough and Denny Seiwell – is well tested after more than one year together; a year full of rehearsals, recording and tour dates. "[This surprise date proved to be] really fantastic, the best we've played up to now," drummer Denny Seiwell says. "We only played an hour or so, but on the tour, we'll be doing a rather extravagant affair, probably playing for two and a half hours. I'm glad we took such a time before starting out on a tour like this, though. It's hard work for a band to come together. It's similar to a marriage, there are the five of you and you have to find out what makes each of you tick, and that learning takes time."[1]

The excitement of Wings' progress as a live band is also palpable for guitarist Henry McCullough, a musician from Joe Cocker's Grease Band and who's very much at home on stage: "It's great. It sounds really good. I mean the band's better live than what it is … like after this next tour we'll be playing things that are better than what's on the album," McCullough reflects. "Wings are a LIVE band and that's the truth. When you go on stage you can't play 75 'My Love's because, you know, you've got to rock and that's something we all know. Like, I know and [Paul] knows that you've to get down and work your arse off. Denny Seiwell is a no shit rock and roll drummer and so he's got all that to come out. See, the band's been through a lot of changes and it's beginning to get right because everybody wanted it to get right. There's been a lot of hard work done."[2]

Wings' British Tour starts a couple of months afterwards. Just a few dates in truth, divided in two legs: a longer one that takes place in May with a string of seventeen concerts, and a short one with only four shows, in the first half of July, added after the great reception to the Spring part of the tour.

And – notwithstanding Seiwell's sneak preview – with a setlist that typically comprises just 15 tracks, compared to the 22 played the previous year on the European Tour. McCartney knows that his homeland audience can be more demanding and so can the press. There's an emblematic episode encompassing the sceptical air that is still breathing around Wings. "One guy came to see a soundcheck and reviewed that as the show," Paul complains. "Saying he didn't think much of Linda's organ playing, when she was in fact playing the piano."[3]

So, he relies on a more balanced repertoire. No room for blues improvisation, with the band focusing on promotion of the recent *Red Rose Speedway*, from which three tracks are performed. Again, no Beatles songs by Lennon/

1973 *Wings' British Tour* poster.

McCartney are played. The running order at the Newcastle concert on 10 July 1973 for example is: "Soily" (already performed during the 1972 *Wings Over Europe Tour*, but still unreleased), "Big Barn Bed", "When the Night", "Wild Life", "Seaside Woman", "Little Woman Love/C Moon", "Live and Let Die", "Maybe I'm Amazed", "My Love", "Go Now", "Say You Don't Mind" (these two sung by Laine), "The Mess", "Hi Hi Hi" and "Long Tall Sally".

To sum up, the setlist features three songs from the recent *Red Rose Speedway*, one each respectively from *McCartney* and *Wild Life*, five tracks that have appeared only on single – including the brand new and explosive "Live and Let Die", the soundtrack to the James Bond movie of the same name, released on 18 June – two still unreleased numbers, a Moody Blues hit, another from Colin Blunstone and a Little Richard classic.

Both critical and public reception are very good. *Rolling Stone* publishes a positive review of the concert held on 12 May at Oxford's New Theatre, along with some interviews with fans. At this point, they identify McCartney as the front man of his new group: "We're a little young to remember the Beatles," a girl in the audience admits. "We've heard of them, but we're here because we're Wings fans."[4]

* * *

On stage, Paul alternates between Rickenbacker bass and electric piano. At this point, the "Ricky" is his new companion: chosen for its solid sound and perhaps also partly out of necessity, since his mythical Höfner was stolen a few months before, on 10 October 1972, in unbelievable circumstances. Ian Horne, one of Wings' roadies, reveals in detail how things went: "In 1972, Paul McCartney was preparing for his first UK and European tours with Wings, and the band was recording their second album, *Red Rose Speedway*. We had rented a truck to move the gear – guitars and amplifiers – to various recording studios and rehearsal spaces across London. We were often criss-crossing London to rehearse or record at Morgan Studios in Willesden Green, the ICA in The Mall, Manticore Studios in Fulham, Island Studios in Notting Hill, and Abbey Road in St John's Wood. One night, after a long day, we got to Notting Hill, where Trevor lived, and decided to park the truck up there for the night. We knew there was a huge padlock on the back doors, but when I got up in the morning and saw the van, with the broken padlock lying in the road, I knew it was bad news. I looked inside and the bass, along with one other guitar and two Vox AC30 amps, had gone. We instantly suspected people living in and around Ladbroke Grove were responsible. One or two people living close by knew that we worked for Paul, so they would have known there was a chance that the kit in the back of the truck belonged to McCartney. We went from door to door, asking people if they'd seen

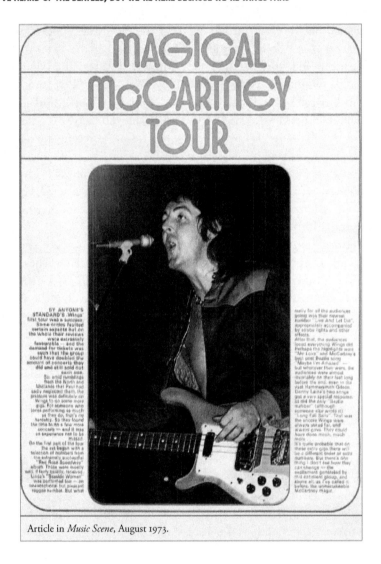

Article in *Music Scene*, August 1973.

anything or if they knew anything, but nobody said a word. I knew it was Paul's original Hofner bass that had been stolen, and I knew what it meant to him. Trevor and I did all we could to find it, but it was gone. Eventually we had to go to Paul's house and tell him that the gear had been stolen from the back of the truck. He told us not to worry, and we kept our jobs. He's a good man, Paul. I worked for him for six years after the bass went missing. But I've carried the guilt all my life."[5]

The event resurfaces in February 2024, when the official Paul McCartney website publishes a brief note, speaking of the recovery of the instrument with these words: "Following the launch of last year's Lost Bass project, Paul's 1961 Höfner 500/1 bass guitar, which was stolen in 1972, has been returned. The guitar has been authenticated by Höfner and Paul is incredibly grateful to all those involved."

Höfner bass or not, avoiding The Beatles' repertoire is a conscious decision for Paul. "We don't want to turn into a second-rate Beatles and be compared to all the groups up and down the Costa Brava," McCartney explains. "I mean, we've come away from all that. Although the others are more keen on The Beatles thing than anyone. Old Denny Laine, he's a total Beatles' freak. In fact, one

Poster for the concert in Newcastle, 10 July 1973.

night one stage he comes up with 'When I was younger so much younger than today'…. And I thought, 'God, there's me trying to get away from it!'"[6]

The alchemy in the band seems right: "We didn't want to tour Britain in a shabby state," Seiwell explains. "But now we're ready. We really shine as a live band."[7]

The tour ends at the City Hall in Newcastle-upon-Tyne on 10 July in front of an audience of 2,000 people. Notwithstanding McCullough's unpredictability – at one point the guitarist falls and plays his guitar solo on "My Love" lying down on stage[8] – the band is a perfectly oiled machine, and the evening is recorded for a possible release as a live album.

✻ ✻ ✻

During the concerts, Wings perform the single "Live and Let Die", another key step in the development of McCartney post-Beatles' career: it is the title song of the latest James Bond film. Relying on the powerful medium of cinema to spread Wings' music is another smart move by McCartney.

Paul knows the popularity of the Bond films and their theme songs well and had flirted with cinema playing a key role in the commercial success of records in the days of The Beatles: "One of John and my ambitions was to write a song for Frank Sinatra," McCartney reveals when talking about the commission for "Live and Let Die." "Another pinnacle was to write a Bond song. It's like an Oscar."[9]

For "Live and Let Die", McCartney returns to George Martin, in the dual role of both arranger and producer. He helps with the orchestral score: "I sort of wrote it, got George round to my house, sat down at the piano, worked out an arrangement with him," Paul says. "Then he went off and scored it. Because I can't do that, I can't voice instruments and stuff. I can in my head, but I don't know how to get it all down. I'll say, tell the cellos to play A, and he'll say, 'Oh, of course, in their range that's a B flat,' or something like that. I can just give him the piano things. So, we worked it up and then we went into the studio and did it in just a couple of days. It was quite easy to do and turned out well for the film."[10]

The result is a high-impact track, built by McCartney and Martin like two experienced filmmakers, mixing pathos, tension and action.

And yet, all of Martin's powers of persuasion are necessary for McCartney's song to be accepted as it is, seemingly because of a misunderstanding, passed on as such by Martin himself. After the recording, the producer goes to meet the Bond executives Harry Saltzman and Albert Broccoli in the Caribbean, where shooting of the film is taking place, bringing with him a cassette recording of the track. When Saltzman hears it, he suggests Shirley Bassey or Thelma Houston as possible performers, maybe referencing the cover version he knew to be part of the soundtrack. A miscommunication, probably: Martin interprets Saltzman's

Promotional ad for "Live and Let Die", *New Musical Express*, 2 June 1973.

words as a request for an alternative to McCartney but holds his ground and is adamant that Paul should have the track.[11]

The single – the B side of which features "I Lie Around", another bucolic McCartney number, sung for the most part by Denny Laine – is a smash: no. 2. in the US (where it goes gold as a million seller), no. 9 in the UK, no. 2 in Canada and Norway, and no. 5 in Australia. "Live and Let Die" also wins a Grammy Award in the "Best Arrangement Accompanying Vocalist" category and receives a 1974 Academy Award nomination in the "Best Original Song" category, although it loses out to "The Way We Were", performed by Barbra Streisand and written by Marvin Hamlisch, and Alan and Marilyn Bergman. The track is also part of the official soundtrack, where a soul version sung by BJ Arnau also appears, probably as a concession to Saltzman.

In other words, McCartney is raising the quality bar. We're on the cusp of something great, lying just around the corner.

Notes

1   Rick Sanders, *Wings: They're all set for take-off!*, *Record Mirror*, 28 April 1973.

2   Ray Telford, *Henry McCullough in The Talk-In*, *Sounds*, 14 April 1973.

3   Chris Welch, *Paul McCartney. The Definitive Biography*, 1984, p. 64.

4   Paul Gambaccini, *Paul McCartney in His Own Words*, 1976, p. 106.

5   Anita Singh, *Sir Paul McCartney's Missing Bass Guitar Was Stolen from a Van, Sound Engineer Reveals*, *The Telegraph*, 27 September 2023. https://www.telegraph.co.uk/news/2023/09/27/paul-mccartney-missing-bass-guitar-stolen-van-notting-hill/

6   Peter Erskine, *They're the Best Band in the Land*, *Disc and Music Echo*, 4 May 1973.

7   Deborah Thomas, *Wings Swing into Spring…*, *Daily Mirror*, p. 11, 17 April 1973.

8   Allan Kozinn–Adrian Sinclair, *The McCartney Legacy. Volume 1: 1969–73*, 2022, p. 594.

9   Garry McGee, *Band on the Run*, 2003, p. 47.

10 Paul Gambaccini, *Paul McCartney in His Own Words*, 1976, p. 71.

11 Allan Kozinn–Adrian Sinclair, *The McCartney Legacy. Volume 1: 1969–73*, 2022, p. 488–489.

— 2 —
TWO LEGS: WINGS SMASHED TO PIECES

I n July 1973 Wings are riding the wave of huge successes, in terms of the audience, the critics and sales. Buoyed up by this acclaim, the band gathers in Scotland on the 31st of that month. The idea is to rehearse new songs for the next album, which Paul wants to record in Lagos, Nigeria.

The trip is set up for the end of August. There are three full working weeks to try out the songs before heading to Africa, and to be able to approach the recordings calmly, thus putting the seal on an intense and important year for the group.

McCartney has already been planning everything for some months. An article published in early May by weekly magazine *Disc and Music Echo* confirms that the recording dates have been finalised and the studio has been booked. Accompanying him in Lagos will be no less than the historic Beatles' engineer, Geoff Emerick. "This was after I'd left Apple. ... As soon as I joined George Martin [at AIR Studios], Paul phoned up and said, 'Do you want to come and do a new album?'" Emerick recalls. "EMI had studios worldwide. There was a list of like fifty studios that EMI had worldwide: India, Pakistan, Russia, Poland and someone just put their finger down with their eyes shut and it stopped at Lagos."[1]

For sure, going to Africa will be no walk in the park. But Paul knows he can count on a trustworthy connection, the ex-drummer of Cream and Blind Faith, Ginger Baker (a virtuoso who has gone down in history as the first "jazz-rock fusion" drummer), who is regularly in Lagos. In fact, he had built his recording studio, Batakota, in the Nigerian capital in January 1973 – although it's established that Wings would use the EMI-owned studio – and he could act as host to the local musicians.

McCartney can also rely on Laine's connections. "I know a lot of the African musicians with Ginger from sessions with Airforce," says Denny. "I was going to go out with him after Airforce. It's all fresh and energetic out there, like it was in New York years ago."[2]

Everything foreshadows a great future for the band.

* * *

But all is not rosy within Wings. "Once or twice, you know we had a few kinda arguments and stuff like 'I don't like the way you do that' and oogh friction."[3]

Regarding the interpersonal dynamics within the band, Paul is practical: "Well, it's a bit democratic but if we're looking for a decision, I'll just make it. But if someone disagrees, it's just ugh ugh, you've got to have disagreements. It's not a living thing unless it's disagreeing."[4]

These tensions are evident to people who have the chance to work in close contact with the band, such as photographer Robert Ellis, who followed Wings during the final part of their European tour in 1972: "McCartney was already dissatisfied with the group format," Ellis reveals, "and it was clear to everybody he was going to change it."[5]

For quite some time, furthermore, there has been discussions about the slim weekly wage (£70) that McCartney gives the others and about the opportunity to set up a contract for Wings' members. It transpires that Paul's income is still blocked because of Apple's legal issues and that, in any case, he has the burden of MPL's staff expenses. All the accumulated discomfort erupts on the afternoon of 14 August.[6] Over the course of the previous two weeks the group has been rehearsing several tracks that will be on the album *Band on the Run*, and that Paul had written for the most part during the first half of the year.

That day, the band is rehearsing "No Words", a song written by Laine that McCartney had helped him finish off. Henry says that the guitar riff, as it is, needs some changes and he has a few ideas. Paul insists that the riff should be played as he wants it to be played. Henry offers a retort. Tempers rise. McCullough, an Irishman of fearless pride, puts his guitar in its case and leaves. "I felt it was time he allowed the musicians to have some of their own ideas used as part of this 'group' vibe. But all that was slowly being lost – the idea from the university tour, the van, the craic and all that started to go out the window," Henry will say.[7]

Paul recalls the incident quite frankly. "We were rehearsing, and I asked him to play a certain bit," he says shortly after. "He was loath to play it and kinda made an excuse about it couldn't be played. I, being a bit of a guitarist myself, knew it could be played and, rather than let it pass, I decided to confront him with it, and we had a confrontation. He left rehearsals a bit choked."[8]

Something has been boiling up for quite a while. McCullough smells a rat regarding his contribution to the band. Paul has a more poppy approach in mind, and the experience of early Wings of playing the blues was instrumental in tackling the first performances in the most natural way possible.

Furthermore, McCullough isn't happy with Linda's contribution to the band. Arguing with the wife of the boss is not a great move. Paul would admit sometime later that Henry left because of that: "'He told me, 'Trying to get things together with a learner in the group didn't work, as far as I'm concerned.'"[9]

Henry McCullough's interview, published in *New Musical Express*, 28 July 1973.

Something may have happened during the tour. Alongside a short article published on *Melody Maker* on 26 May, just before the last date of *Wings' British Tour*, the magazine writes: "Reports that Henry McCullough was to leave Wings were described this week as 'nonsense'". It seems like a classic denial to silence the rumours.

Some weeks later, McCullough seems to signal a different message in an interview with *New Musical Express*, with some MPL staff also present. "I mean, I've never been the kind of guitarist to play twenty-minute solos anyway," says

Henry. "I don't feel restricted or anything like that. I think it's also down to the numbers we're playing. They're quite highly structured, not very free, and on stage I'm just playing what I play on the record. Perhaps I would like the band to be a little freer. It's just been kept that way so far. But I could never be just Paul McCartney's backing guitarist. I'd leave if it was like that."[10]

Maybe in order to mitigate this statement, McCullough in general comes across as being happy with how things are evolving, although there's no doubting the fact that Paul's personality is dominant. "I want to contribute as well," continues the musician firmly. "I think it's coming though. Over the last eighteen months we've had to sort out the slight differences we had musically. At the start, I wasn't really aware of what I was doing. It only came after I got to know the lads in the band. Now I think Wings have reached the point where music is really starting to come out of the band. Everybody's contributing and the results are a five-piece product. That's what it's getting to and it's great. Obviously, it'll always be Paul McCartney's group, but we've worked out of this system where it was just 'Paul McCartney and his group Wings'."[11]

It could be that McCullough is safeguarding himself. Because, when, shortly afterwards, what he foresaw would happen does indeed come to pass – that is to say, his lack of artistic freedom, the forced execution of ideas – he's a man of his word and leaves the band. News of Wings' guitarist leaving is out in a few days, and obviously there's a communication strategy to be set up: official statements, counterstatements, quashing rumours.

Henry, according to the MPL archives, officially leaves Wings on 25 August. "[He] rang up to say he was leaving," Paul would recall.[12] A spokesman for the band announces that McCullough is leaving because of "musical differences and by mutual agreement with the rest of the band." Some press reports blow the situation up, and rumours spread that Paul and Henry had come to blows: "There was no row when Henry left," says Linda, with whom McCullough does not have the best relationship. "Somebody picked that up, but it's not true. When Henry left, we thought, 'Right, fair enough'."[13]

* * *

Lacking a lead guitarist only two weeks before the planned trip to Lagos could have been a big problem. But not for McCartney, who is a "frustrated guitarist", as the saying goes. During his career, he pulled out key solos, such as in "Taxman" and "Maybe I'm Amazed", and he has played many lead parts on *RAM* and *Wild Life*. So, he takes on the role himself.

In truth, drummer Denny Seiwell is worried. Realising that Paul isn't intending to replace the guitarist, Seiwell senses a situation similar to *RAM*, where there were endless overdubs, and he knows that at least for some time, the band's live

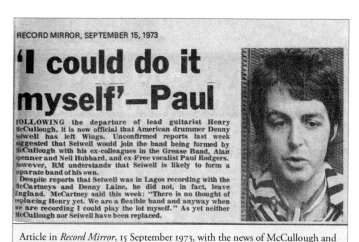

RECORD MIRROR, SEPTEMBER 15, 1973

'I could do it myself'–Paul

FOLLOWING the departure of lead guitarist Henry McCullough, it is now official that American drummer Denny Seiwell has left Wings. Unconfirmed reports last week suggested that Seiwell would join the band being formed by McCullough with his ex-colleagues in the Grease Band, Alan Spenner and Neil Hubbard, and ex-Free vocalist Paul Rodgers. However, RM understands that Seiwell is likely to form a separate band of his own.

Despite reports that Seiwell was in Lagos recording with the McCartneys and Denny Laine, he did not, in fact, leave England. McCartney said this week: "There is no thought of replacing Henry yet. We are a flexible band and anyway when we are recording I could play the lot myself." As yet neither McCullough nor Seiwell have been replaced.

Article in *Record Mirror*, 15 September 1973, with the news of McCullough and Seiwell leaving Wings.

activity would stop. For a start, Wings' participation in the Italian Festivalbar, planned for 25 August in Asiago, is cancelled.

Seiwell talks with Paul, but to no avail. "I begged him to get another guitar player and rehearse for a month," he recalls. "So, we could down there with a hot band and cut the record live. But he didn't want to do that, so I left."[14]

It is on 30 August, the day planned for the African trip, that Denny announces that he has had enough. "The night that we were going to Lagos, there was a car [sent by Paul] in front of my place, and I just thought, 'You know what? I've got to put an end to this.'" Seiwell recalls. "I just said, 'That's it, I think I'm going to leave.' I'm in one of the top bands in the world, and we're living in a dingy, one-bedroom, furnished apartment. It was just really a rat hole. I picked up the phone and called Paul, and I said, 'I'm done. I can't do this anymore.' It was hard to do, really, extremely hard to do. And he was shocked."[15]

More than this, when the drummer announces that he is leaving the band, Paul and Linda are furious. But Seiwell is unmoved: "I left because of financial matters," Denny admits. "Henry [McCullough] had just left. Henry left when we were up in Scotland. Here we were getting ready to go to Lagos and cut *Band on the Run* and we still had no agreement in writing. We had a verbal agreement that didn't hold any water. I'd already made *Wild Life* and *Red Rose Speedway* with that agreement in mind, but I never received a dime from that. It became a financial matter at that point and the fact that we weren't getting that document, letter of agreement, that never came. I said, 'You know what? This is not good. My interests are not being looked after here.' I should have sat him down and talked to him and said, 'Look, I won't do this anymore!' But instead, I was infuriated by a couple of things that happened and I just called him up and said, 'I'm leaving. I'm done here.'"[16]

This adds a further challenge to McCartney's mood, as if that were needed. But drums hold no fear for him. He already played them for The Beatles, replacing Ringo when he temporarily left during the "White Album" sessions, and obviously also on his debut album. Paul has not fully mastered them, but he's got a certain approach, and knows how to manage in the recording studio to overcome any difficulties. So, he's going to be Wings' drummer.

Laine is diplomatic when asked about the two departures. "I really don't know why Henry and Denny decided to leave," Denny explains to a journalist. "Perhaps part of it is due to the pace that Paul works or perhaps it was because they felt their creativity was being stifled. If it was the latter, there was certainly no need for it because Paul always encouraged us to contribute whatever we felt we could. Paul worked really hard in trying to keep the band together. He certainly never wanted either Henry of Denny to leave."[17]

The die is cast. The first Wings five-member lineup has lasted eighteen months. From now on, for Paul it is all about to demonstrating to those who have quit that, after all, he can manage without them, and to himself that the moment has come to get serious.

It will be so. "I was bloody annoyed," Paul would say years later. "I suppose I could have said, 'Oh all right, we won't go', but it was more like, 'Screw you, I'll make an album you will want to have been on.' I still know the guys now – actually I talked to Denny today – and they both regret not going." [18]

Notes

1   Greg Schmidt, *The Victor Company | Geoff Emerick (EMI/HMV/Beatles) | His Master's Voice: Music Industry Interviews*, 18 January 2023, https://www.youtube.com/watch?v=C6czTmxnH_4.

2   Peter Erskine, *Denny Laine it all on the line…*, Disc and Music Echo, 4 May 1973,

3   Peter Harvey, *Paul's Wings find their identity on stage*, Record Mirror, 21 July 1973.

4   Peter Harvey, *Paul's Wings find their identity on stage*, Record Mirror, 21 July 1973.

5   Chris Welch, *Paul McCartney. The Definitive Biography*, 1984, p. 65.

6   Alan Kozinn–Adrian Sinclair, *The McCartney Legacy. Volume 1: 1969–73*, 2022, p. 603.

7   Colin Harper, *Hello Goodbye - Henry McCullough & Wings*, Mojo, September 1997, p. 162.

8   Chris Welch, *Onwards and upwards*, Melody Maker, 1 December 1973.

9   *Lay Off Linda, Says Her Off-Key Paul*, Sunday Mirror, 25 November 1973.

10 James Johnson, *H. McCullough meets the Wings Fan Club*, New Musical Express, 28 July 1973.

11 James Johnson, *H. McCullough meets the Wings Fan Club*, New Musical Express, 28 July 1973.

12 Chris Welch, *Onwards and upwards*, Melody Maker, 1 December 1973.

13 Julie Webb, *Wings in the Air*, New Musical Express, 27 October 1973.

14 Robyn Flans, *Denny Seiwell. Finding His Wings*, Modern Drummer, November 2001, p. 24.

15 Alan Kozinn–Adrian Sinclair, *The McCartney Legacy. Volume 1: 1969–73*, 2022, p. 606.

16 http://www.classicbands.com/DennySeiwellInterview.html

17 Mike Beatty, *Denny's writing a whole lot more*, Record Mirror, 12 January 1974.

18 Phil Hogan, *Paul McCartney: "Suddenly it just all came together"*, The Guardian, 7 November 2010.

— 3 —
LAGOS: A JINXED TOWN

P aul and Linda leave from London on the evening of Thursday, 30 August and land in Lagos the following day. McCartney has chosen Nigeria based on a postcard image of the country.

"Sometimes you just get bored, and you think, 'I'm going into the same studio,' and you think it'll make the album boring," Paul is to recall about the reason behind that choice. "So, I had a few ideas for songs that I was quite keen on, so I asked EMI where they had studios around the world. And they sent over a note, and it said Rio de Janeiro, there was China, of all places, and all these amazing countries where they had studios, and Lagos, in Nigeria. I thought, 'Lagos! Africa! Rhythms!' Because I've always liked the African music ... I liked the idea of going to a place that had produced records that had had great rhythms."[1]

Not only a naive view, but also uninformed. Nigeria, which had been part of the British Commonwealth first as a protectorate (1901) and later as a colony (1914), until it became independent in 1960, had faced a civil war that started in 1967 after the Biafra region's declaration of independence and that had ended only in 1970. What's more, it had been suffocated by Yakubu Gowon's regime, instituted in 1966 after a military coup. The sanitary condition of the city is dire, and EMI send a message to McCartney: "Would advise against your going there as there's just been an outbreak of cholera." Paul would only receive the message on his return.

In truth, other and more prosaic reasons seem behind the choice: "It just happened to be the only EMI studio available during this three-week period," Paul would say.[2]

But selecting the capital of Nigeria is not a last-minute thing. Many elements make us think that McCartney has had the African scenario on his radar for quite some time.

Laine knew ex-drummer of Cream Ginger Baker very well. Baker's group Air Force had included him in its lineup the year in 1970. Baker was a pioneer in the discovery of the emerging musical movement called Afro-beat. He's the one who invites Fela Kuti's band Africa '70 to London's Abbey Road Studios in the summer of 1971. Furthermore, engineer Tony Clark had been in Africa shortly before and he mentions to Paul the magic of that environment during the sessions for Wings' *Wild Life*.[3] Last but not least, it should be noted that a group named The Wings, led by Spud Nathan, had been founded around 1970 in Lagos.

And it seems a certain fashion for recording in exotic locations has become common practice in recent years. In November 1972, the Rolling Stones went to Dynamic Sound Studio in Kingston, Jamaica, for the recording of their album *Goats Head Soup*. In January 1973, it is Elton John's turn, but his experience in the same studio for the sessions for *Goodbye Yellow Brick Road* aren't positive. Various reasons, including the substandard conditions of the microphones and of the recording system (something similar to what McCartney would experiment in Lagos) soon led Elton and his band to stop working there. "We did a version of 'Saturday Night's (Alright for Fighting)' that sounded like a bunch of angry bees," guitarist Davey Johnstone recalled. "It sounded terrible."[4]

Therefore, the true story of this choice is a puzzle with a thousand pieces and is still to be written in full.

On the flight to Nigeria, Paul senses that a real adventure is starting. "Before we got there, we are in the plane, the pilot had recognised me and said, 'If you like to come in and watch the landing …' So, I said, 'Uh, lovely'. I'm up there watching the landing and down below is jungle and there's a mist on the jungle It's perfect, it's Africa! But the two pilots were going, 'Can you see it?' 'I think that's it, over there,' 'No'. I thought, 'Oh my God, are we even going to land?' We did! The impression was that it is very underdeveloped. It was a bit of a shock."[5]

Denny Laine and Geoff Emerick have been in Lagos since the day before. The engineer had to overcome his entomophobia before deciding to go: his experience in the studio would prove fundamental. The impact of the Nigerian capital on the engineer is cataclysmic. In the car on the way to the studio, Emerick notes a number of people walking along the side of the road wrapped in bandages and sheets. Before he says anything, the driver reads his thoughts: "Those are lepers."[6]

The accommodation is worse than imagined. Emerick stays in a villa with Laine and the two roadies Ian Horne and Trevor Jones but, after Denny's pranks with insects and close encounters of the third kind with the local fauna (principally salamanders), Geoff asks to be moved to a hotel downtown. But things are little better there, with rooms infested with cockroaches.

* * *

To the less than idyllic climatic conditions, we must also add the professional ones – and they're equally difficult. In Apapa, the suburb of Lagos where EMI has its studio, is also Ginger Baker, and further troubles emerge. Before leaving, the instructions are clear: the EMI studio has to be used, thus avoiding any additional costs. Nevertheless, Paul plans to record with Ginger, but EMI representatives allow no interference.

Baker is disappointed because, after all, the McCartney trip to Africa is thanks to him. But the idea that Paul would have used his studio is probably the result of a misunderstanding. "An American representative for Paul McCartney [Vincent Romeo] had a look around and was very impressed," Baker recalls. "I was knocked out because a booking from Paul would really put us on the map. Through our contacts in the government, we arranged for Paul, Linda, Denny and the rest of Wings to get visas to come to Nigeria. I am fuckin' angry. The actual truth of the matter is that *Band on the Run* would never have been recorded if it wasn't for me."[7]

McCartney himself seems to sense that the general vibe is not good. "When we arrived there, we found that some people were treating our visit as some sort of bad luck omen," Paul admits. "Really strange."[8]

The impressions of the EMI studio aren't the best. The studio is located on Wharf Road no. 7, a busy main road that runs along the city harbour, once the scene of frequent loading of slaves en route to Liverpool. Not by chance, there remains today a Liverpool Road nearby, in "memory" of the commercial relationships between the two cities.

At EMI, Emerick can rely on a studio manager, Odion Iruoje, and two assistants, Monday Oki – who later on would be in charge of the studio when it would move from Apapa to Ikeja, with the setup of a 24-track machine[9] – and Innocent. The equipment at the EMI studio is in a parlous state. The recording studio itself is unfinished and there are neither a drum booth nor acoustic screens. Iruoje doesn't understand. "The studio was a decent size, and there were the required amount of cabling and mic stands, but there was no drum booth," Emerick recalls. "In fact, there were no acoustic screens whatsoever. It took a while for me to explain what acoustic screens were and why we needed them. When we arrived the next morning, a crew of workmen were indeed hard at work building screens. At one point even Paul picked up a saw and began sawing wood. By the third day or so, they were all done … except that the carpenters had left an empty hole in the middle of each screen! They couldn't understand why the screens had to be filled in with a sheet of glass in order to block the sound. We lost a few days of recording time as a result."[10]

Quite an unusual situation, to say the least. "When we first went to have a look at the studio, there was about four or five black carpenters who were building booths because they don't use them out there apparently," Paul reveals. "These guys were boppin' about to a record and smoking some native weed, I think. Some guy had probably said, 'Hey man, these Westerners are coming, and they use booths …'"[11]

So, the start is a tale of apprenticeship in carpentry. "It turned out to be an unbuilt studio, but it was enough, and we helped to construct vocal booths and things. It became part of the fun. No, I didn't actually get a hammer out myself, but they got carpenters in, and we told them what we needed – a big wooden box with a door in it and Perspex windows. They just didn't have vocal booths. I suppose they were used to recording live African bands rather than suave westerners."[12]

Emerick is shocked when he does the inventory of the equipment. "A few dozen mics were strewn about haphazardly; not one of them was stored inside its protective case," the engineer reveals. "There were a couple of decent Neumanns in there, but the rest of the microphones were run-of-the-mill, inexpensive models."[13]

The recording desk is an EMI TG12345. This eight-channel console, mostly the outcome of the engineering genius of Mike Bachelor, had been introduced at the end of the Sixties, replacing the four-track machines (REDD.37 and REDD.51) at that point exploited to their limits. The main innovation was the presence of a limiter/compressor in each channel.[14]

In the traditional style of London's Abbey Road studios, everything is set up to guarantee the smoothest transition possible. In early summer 1968, the first TG console is installed in a rehearsal room (no. 65) so that the engineers could gain experience with it. Its clean sound would characterise the *Abbey Road* album, the first recorded by The Beatles using the new console. And then, albums such as Ringo's *Sentimental Journey* and Harrison's *All Things Must Pass*. Or Lennon's single "Instant Karma!" and some of McCartney's tracks for his first solo record ("Maybe I'm Amazed" and "Every Night").

Over five years, technical requirements have changed considerably, but in Lagos, technology is not in step with the times. Emerick seems aware of it. "Sixteen-track recording was state-of-the-art in 1973 [EMI wasn't exactly the quickest in following the market evolution and 16-track consoles had already appeared at Island Studios and Trident Studios in 1970, while at Abbey Road they had to wait until spring 1972 for all studios to be equipped[15]], but I knew it would be too much to expect to find that in the Lagos studio," the engineer recalls. "I asked to see the multitrack machine. It was eight-track, which was fine, but then Monday went on to explain that it only had four 'sync' amps. These were the electronic components that allowed you to listen to prerecorded tracks off the record head. What was meant was that I could only ever play back four tracks when we were overdubbing. Yes, I could choose which four tracks I wanted the musicians to hear … but it was still quite a limitation."[16]

The reason is easily explained: "overdubbing" is not a well-known concept in African music culture. It's hard to imagine that Emerick was not informed in advance about the recording desk; anyway, the simultaneous playback of only four tracks is a serious obstacle even for a professional like him.

At least the studio initially provides Paul with inspiration for a possible title for his future album. "The funny thing is," McCartney recalls, "there was a plaque next to it, which advertised a local carpenter. It read, 'Son of always.'"[17] He toys with this title for a while, but then he rules it out. If you think about it, it would have been an epic title, in line with the timeless quality of the record.

The title *Band on the Run* comes later. "'Band on the Run' was always going to be the big, epic track on the album," Paul said, "but I didn't necessarily know it was going to be the title. But it eventually comes to the surface, and I thought, 'Well, that's an obvious title. That's the one.'"[18]

*　*　*

Having overcome the technical deficiencies of the EMI studio, sessions commence as planned on Monday, 3 September 1973: they will last two complete working weeks, until Friday 14 September. "We were there for three weeks, and we recorded seven tracks," McCartney says at the time.[19] As shown in a photo of the original eight-track Lagos tape box,[20] six tracks are committed to tape in Apapa, in the following order – "Mamunia", "Band on the Run", "Helen Wheels", "Mrs. Vandebilt", "No Words" and "Let Me Roll It" – while a seventh, "Picasso's Last Words" is recorded on 17 September at Ginger Baker's Batakota Studio:[21] a courtesy gesture, in an attempt to tone down the tension that has mounted over the use of the recording studios.

With Wings' line-up reduced its bare bones, McCartney lays down the basic tracks in the only way possible: he plays drums, while Laine provides rhythm guitar and Linda adds Moog and organ.

Paul tries to work out the drum parts, and he does it by making up for his partial lack of technical skills with fantasy and … some trickery. Overall, McCartney puts aside his tendency to overdo things and does only what serve the song. "When our drummer left, there was a kind of 'I'll show you' aspect," Paul confesses. "And I thought, 'Okay well now I don't have to tell him how I want the drums.' And I'm ok drummer, I'm not a great drummer but I've got a style, I've got a feel. So, I kept it simple. The drums on *Band on the Run* are pretty simple."[22]

McCartney explains the two main reasons why he decided to do it by himself. The first is linked to his admiration for one of his musical idols, who proved to be an inspiration. "I thought, If Stevie Wonder could do it, so could I," Paul says about his choice to drum on the album.[23] The second reason is more practical: "I didn't want to break in an African drummer 'cos it would have taken hours to tell him exactly what I wanted."[24]

On close inspection, various gimmicks are scattered throughout the whole album to help Paul. "Mamunia" lacks a drum part, featuring only Laine on congas, while a roadie beats the bass drum; for the shuffle tempo on "Helen Wheels" − a rhythm that Paul always found tricky and one he will never learn properly − McCartney is helped again by Laine, with "combined provisions" formed by Denny on bass drum and himself on snare and cymbals. In a photo included in the *Band on the Run* booklet, you can also see McCartney on his knees beating the bass drum with a stick, an expedient he would resort to on other occasions during his career.

To help Paul try to keep a steady beat, a rhythm box is also employed, very likely the Korg Mini Pops MP-7, built in different models since the end of the Sixties: it can be heard distinctively on "No Words" (where Macca shows a little uncertainty in keeping the beat) and on "Picasso's Last Words", where the percussion department also includes Ginger Baker and where the drum part is minimal, as it is, after all, on "Let Me Roll It".

"I think the drumming on *Band on the Run* is quite good," Paul admits with some pride. "There's nothing flash. But I can hold a good beat. I like drumming anyway, so Denny not turning up gave me a chance to fulfil an ambition. I always suggested Ringo things that he might play. I hear drums well. In Hamburg, I used to drum when Tony Sheridan's drummer was sick. I did for a week for the extra cash."[25]

Notwithstanding the technical limitations of the studio, Emerick finds that this had a positive impact on the sound. "The sound is the person playing," the engineer explains. "Sometimes it's a plus to be away from the studio and that studio sound. Sometimes those little rooms can give a recording a special character. I always loved Paul's drumming. He has a great sense of timing. When The Beatles were working on drum parts, it was always Paul working it out with Ringo."[26]

The presence of Laine to lay down the basic track is what allows McCartney to conceive and execute his rhythm parts with a degree of serenity: "We would put the track down that way where he could get the drum part first," Laine explains. "That's how it worked on that album, and I think that's how we got the specific feel for *Band on the Run*."[27]

Before the recording starts in earnest, however, Paul and Denny lay down a sort of acoustic demo. "It was a very slim background," McCartney recalls. "It was me on drums, or probably normally it would be me and Denny starting off on a couple of acoustics, so to get the song down, like you would for a demo. We just built it up like a sculpture."[28]

They make a virtue out of necessity. "We did it almost as though it was a home recording," Laine says. "A lot of the equipment that was out there really wasn't workable. It was all hand-me-downs from EMI, and they really didn't know what they were doing. And we kept it basic. No frills." [29]

Linda, for her part, puts into practice what she learned: "On the album I play piano [she may mean electric piano] and Moog and Paul plays the drums – he's quite fantastic. I didn't really have any musical training. Just musical appreciation. Paul had taught me a lot and Denny, too. I had piano lessons as a kid, but I never practised."[30]

* * *

In a possible attempt to take advantage of Africa's musical environment and culture and fill out the sound of the group, abandoned as it was by two of its five elements, McCartney also considers involving local musicians, mainly for percussion. But his desire to use African personnel wanes when Fela Ransome-Kuti, a leading figure of the Afrobeat movement – a style of music he contributed to creating, and based on a fusion of jazz, funk, highlife, and traditional Nigerian, African chants and rhythms – and local activist, considered a sort of king in his country, stages a protest in the Lagos press.

Fela and Paul were close in July 1971, when Fela is at Abbey Road at the same time as McCartney is there to record Wings' debut album *Wild Life*: Fela is in the studio on 24 and 25 July, the first two days of sessions for McCartney's band.

Fela's two historic sessions happen at the suggestion of late engineer Tony Clark. Jeff Jarratt, the producer of those recordings, remembers it well: "He suggested to Mike Wells that if he did bring Fela to London, he should ask me to produce the sessions. I had heard some of Fela's music and his pioneering Afrobeat sound on the John Peel radio show and when Mike asked me to be involved the opportunity of starting my production career with such an exciting artist seemed almost too good to be true – especially when he said that Ginger Baker would be guesting on some of the recordings. This is something I shall forever be grateful to Tony for."[31]

Fela and his Africa '70 band land in London on the evening of 23 July and the following day they enter the studio early, setting up their equipment: "From the moment they started playing we knew that this was going to be something special," Jarrat says. "It was unusually cold for the time of year and to begin with several of the band members were struggling with the change of temperature between London and Nigeria. It was particularly difficult for the three conga players whose hands were stinging as they played their complex rhythms."[32]

Relying on the brand new 16-track desk (the TG12345 MK IV) installed at the time only in Studio Three, Fela and his band record two albums in two days:

on Saturday, 24 July they commit to tape *Afrodisiac*, while Sunday, 25 July it's the turn of *Live!* (featuring Ginger Baker), recorded live before an audience of just 150 people, including guests and authorised personnel. Paul and Wings, who had a very productive Saturday afternoon by recording four tracks of their future album, look in on the evening session by Africa '70.

* * *

If Paul could not take full advantage of Fela's presence at Abbey Road, being so busy recording, in Lagos everything seems perfect for a meeting with all the trimmings.

In theory, it's the ideal opportunity to seal the admiration of McCartney for the African musician. In practice, things go differently. The location is a club called Afrika Shrine, owned by Fela: founded by him in 1972, it was modelled in part on the Mbari Artists and Writers Club in the university city of Ibadan, both a place of entertainment and a cultural and political salon. Here, on Friday, 14 September Paul goes to listen to the marvels of African music – and not only of music, since he's offered "the strongest joint I've ever had".[33]

Although McCartney recalled that Fela had invited him to the club,[34] it was instead Ginger Baker who told Paul about the show. It seemed a good occasion to finalise his mediator role between two great musicians and two musical cultures. Kuti's side of the story, as told by French screenwriter and musician Lou-lou Dédola, who often visited Fela since the late Eighties, is different: "Actually, McCartney called him on the phone, and he said, 'Hi, it's me, Paul McCartney! I'd like to do a duet with you,'" Dédola relates. "And Fela said to him, 'Who? I don't know who you are.'"[35]

In any case, the performance is something unforgettable. "When Fela and his band eventually began to play, after a long, crazy buildup, I just couldn't stop weeping with joy," McCartney would confess. "It was such a fantastic sound, to hear this African band playing right up your nose, because we were sitting right by them. The rhythm section was so hot, so unusual, that it was a very moving experience for me."[36]

It's such a moving and intense experience, that McCartney still remembers some of the music played there, although unable to name track he was so impressed with. "It was one of the most amazing musical moments of my life, cause the band was so unbelievable," he recalled in 2013. "This is going to be my favourite Fela's song. I'm not sure there's a record of it."[37] Based on the riff Paul plays on his electric piano during the video of his interview while remembering Fela Kuti, the song is undoubtedly "Why Black Men Dey Suffer?".

During a break, the atmosphere suddenly becomes tense. Some musicians approach McCartney aggressively. Kuti tries to calm down the waters and invites

Paul on stage, and the two hold their hands high.[38] Paul had been thinking of recruiting some local musician, something that would have guaranteed some more well-deserved media exposure to African music: "Except for things like, 'Soul Makossa', they don't really get heard in the West,"[39] McCartney observes.

But when Paul goes backstage and starts a discussion to see if any musicians would be interested in taking part in his recording, Fela's mood changes and the ex-Beatle soon understands that it's time to leave. The next day, Fela shows up at the EMI studio surrounded by his bodyguards. Paul is accused of wanting to steal African music, sampling its rhythms and sounds as if it was a form of "white artistic colonialism". Trying to salvage the situation, McCartney plays Fela the tapes, to reassure him that the music had no African influences at all. Paul tries to make him understand he doesn't need to steal anything: "I had to say, 'Do us a favour, Fela. We do all right as it is, actually. We sell a couple of records here and there'."[40]

The incident becomes quite serious. "It was a lot of misunderstanding," Linda would explain. "We met Fela through Ginger [Baker] who has a studio over there, and one night we went down to *The Shrine*, a club that Kela has. Anyway, he used to come by the studios, and it was all very friendly and then one day he came by with a lot of heavies and sort of sat Paul down and said, 'You're stealing our music'. And Paul said, 'I'm not. Come and listen to the tracks. I haven't used any of your musicians.'"[41]

Kuti's suspicious attitude, truth to be told, has some roots. Only a couple of months before McCartney's arrival, South-African trumpet player Hugh Masekela had landed in Lagos, and he recorded the album *Introducing Hedzoleh Soundz* at EMI studio along with a band from Ghana who were introduced to him by Kuti himself sometime before. Fela uses this misunderstanding with Paul as the basis for wanting to understand more in-depth Paul's presence in Africa. It seems that he couldn't tolerate the blend of influences in Masekela's record. "The trouble was, Hugh Masekela went there and used an African band," McCartney says. "And they did the same thing to him, you know. 'You're not going to take our music back and exploit it?' and Hugh said 'No' and he did."[42]

Not leaving anything to chance, however, Fela speaks to radios and newspapers again about the potential musical theft, and the following day the newspaper *Lagos Evening Times* publishes an article with the sinister title: "Step Softly, This Town Is Jinxed".

Do things return to normality between McCartney and Fela after that? It seems so, although there is no evidence of another meeting between the two in following years. Back from Africa, Paul shows enthusiasm for Kuti's music, wielding his album *Shakara* during some press interviews. "Have you heard this album?" McCartney asks the reporter. "It's the Nigerian fella who was on the

Ginger Baker program, he's great, very funky. It's incredible, this guy actually lives with all these women, a kind of harem …"[43]

And there are essentially no examples of any blending of McCartney's and African music, with only one exception, which is moreover related to an unreleased song, "Waterspout", widely bootlegged over the decades and considered by many the best Paul track that's still on the shelf. The tribal rhythm, filled with percussion, recalls almost to the letter that of the aforementioned "Why Black Men Dey Suffer?", which appeared on Kuti's album of the same name in 1971, and which Paul had heard at Kuti's show at The Shrine during that unforgettable – in many senses – evening.

❋   ❋   ❋

At least, Paul and Linda have been able to relax somewhat during the previous weekends, visiting the tenure of Chief Moshood Abiola, one of the most important and richest Nigerian entrepreneurs, at that time head of ITT, a company in the transport and infrastructure business. Abiola jokes with Paul: "Mac, why you no have four wives?' 'One's enough trouble, Chief," McCartney replies.[44]

The Lagos misadventures do not end with the musical and artistic misunderstanding with Kuti, but also involve the aspect of personal security. One night, Paul and Linda – the only white people on the streets – found themselves surrounded by a group and are robbed at knifepoint: McCartney hands over all that he has, including cameras and a tape recorder, apparently including some demos.

It's a key episode, at least from the perspective of Paul's narration of *Band on the Run* over the decades. Did the portable recorder contain a cassette with music or other types of recordings instead? Paul has always referred, generically, to demos. Are these the demos taped by Wings in Scotland? Or the acoustic demos that Paul usually prepares ahead the sessions, and that serve as a guide for the band rehearsals?

McCartney would often relate this episode to enthral the press and colour the African trip, saying he had to remember the songs in order to rerecord them: in truth, as we will see, the robbery happens on 17 September, when the sessions are nearly complete, and anyway after all seven pieces have been already recorded. In the archives, there's no trace of any remakes and, until his flight back to London, on 22 September, Paul does not record anything further. And even though the tape containing Wings' rehearsals was stolen, certainly the original master would be available somewhere in the UK.

It's interesting to follow how the narrative of this episode evolves over the course of decades. In the many interviews done on the spur of the moment for the promotion of the album, McCartney only mentions it on two occasions, the first to *Melody Maker*, with these words: "And we got robbed while we were down there. Some guys robbed us – with a knife. We got held up walking out at night – you're not supposed to do that. They took our tape recorder and cameras and gear."[45]

The reference is to a tape recorder but not specifically to a tape. It's plausible a tape was inserted in it, while it's less plausible that the tape would contain recorded music, which would have made more sense to keep in the studio. Perhaps, Paul decides to carry a recorder on the hunt for sounds and noises that he could judge to be of interest, or just keep it to hand should a melody buzz into his head.

In the second case, Paul talks of the robbery in an interview for the newspaper *Tina*, introducing a small but fundamental element, the timing, with which

Article in *Tina*, 17 November 1973.

May 1973. - Wings British Tour.

June 1st - "Live and Let Die" single released.

June 18th - *Paul's* 31st birthday.

July 6th - London Premiere of "Live and Let Die". Starring Roger Moore

August 25 - Henry McCullough leaves Wings.

August 30th - Denny Seiwell leaves Wings.
         Paul and Linda and Denny Lane leave for Lagos to record
  , m   at E.M.I. Studios.

Sept. 1st - "Live and Let Die" - gold disc in U.S.A.

Sept 17th - Paul attacked and robbed in Lagos.

Sept 22nd - Paul, Linda and Denny return from Lagos.

Sept 24th - Linda's 31st birthday.

Oct 12th - "Helen Wheels"/"Country Dreamer" released in U.S.A.

Oct 19th - "Helen Wheels"/"Country Dreamer" released in Britain.

Oct 29th - Denny Lane's 29th Birthday.

Nov   - Ringo L.P. released, featuring tracks from John, Paul and
         George, track entitled "6 O'Clock" written by Paul and Linda.

Nov 14th - Paul and Linda

MPL internal memo, which reports the date of the robbery in Lagos (with kind permission of Adrian Sinclair).

we'll deal shorty after: "Then *just before we left*, we had a rather funny experience," McCartney explains. "Linda and I were wandering along this rather deserted road, when this car drew up. We thought at first that the guys inside were just offering us a lift, when suddenly one of them pulled a knife on us and threatened our lives if we didn't hand over the money. Naturally enough, we didn't much feel like messing around, and so they got the money."[46]

So, Paul hints at when the robbery took place but regarding what was stolen, he only refers to money. No cassettes, no cameras.

The circumstance of the robbery, on the contrary, is strangely not event hinted at in the lengthy interview with Paul Gambaccini published on *Rolling Stone* (which also dedicates its cover to McCartney) in January 1974. A wide-ranging discussion, where Paul explores practically all his career up to that moment, and where the section dedicated to *Band on the Run* has a particular importance.

In 1977, Paul goes back to the timing detail, escaped by almost everybody. When did this robbery really take place? It's the heart of the matter because, beyond the content of the stolen cassette along with the recorder, it contradicts the theory of the songs having to be remembered. "We had been in Lagos *a couple of weeks*," Paul said. "Linda and I had set off like a couple of tourists, loaded with tapes and cameras, to walk to Denny's house, which was about twenty minutes down the road. A car pulls up beside us. Then a guy gets out and I thought that he wanted to give us a lift … It stopped again. Then one of them, there were about five or six black guys, rolled down the window and asked, 'Are you a traveller?' I said, 'No, we are just out for a little walk. It's a holiday and we are tourists,' giving the whole game away. So, with that, all the doors of the car flew open, and they all came out and one of them had a knife. Their eyes were wild, and Linda was screaming, 'He's a musician, don't kill him'."[47]

The reference to the mugging is also mentioned in the interview with Vic Garbarini, published in August 1980 in *Musician* magazine and later in February 1981 in the album *The McCartney Interview*. In this case, Paul frames it within the unfortunate circumstances of the recordings of *Band on the Run,* but he doesn't add any further details.

In the book taken from the movie *Give My Regards to Broad Street* (1984), the reference to the episode is only in a brief passage: "I was mugged and the day after I fainted". It's interesting to note in this case that the two events, the robbery and the fainting (of which more later) are mentioned in succession, almost to establish a link between them: as if the stress deriving from such a dangerous incident had found its way out on a physical disease.

In 1986, during the interview with BBC journalist Richard Skinner, included in the home video *The Paul McCartney Special,* released in junction with the promotion of the album *Press to Play,* Paul only hints at it: "I was mugged one night."[48]

The first suggestion of music being contained on the tape seems to be in 1988. The occasion is a lengthy interview on Paul's solo career, in conjunction with the release of the compilation *All the Best!* "We got mugged out in Lagos," Paul relates. "Linda and I were on foot, in the middle of the darkest Africa, and we got mugged one night, and they took all this stuff – a lot of tapes, the demos of the songs!"[49] This time, McCartney talks about cassettes and recordings, specifying the content: demos.

The same story is reported sometime later in *Club Sandwich,* Paul's official magazine at the time. Speaking about the songs on *All the Best!,* McCartney says the following statement about "Band on the Run": "One night me and Linda got mugged. We'd been told not to walk around, but in those days, we were slightly hippie – 'Hey, don't worry'. About five fellers jumped out of a car and one of them had a knife, so all my tapes went. These were all the songs I'd written, so I had to try and remember them all. The joke is, I'm sure the fellers who took them wouldn't know what they were. They probably chucked them away, so lying in some Nigerian jungle there's little cassettes of *Band on the Run*."[50]

On this occasion, Paul adds that the mugging determines the fact that he has to remember the song in order to record them (which is not true, as we saw) and talks about the destiny of the tapes.

The same story is aired in 1989. Again, the context is another retrospective on his solo career, broadcast during the spring of that year over eight episodes with the title *McCartney on McCartney*. Around the corner, there are both the release of the new album *Flowers in the Dirt* and the *Paul McCartney World Tour* that will start in autumn, his first in thirteen years. The words are basically the same, with only slight differences, additions or omissions. "I've written some of them, but one night we got mugged," Paul says. "We've been told not to walk around, but we got mugged … Five guys jumped out of a car, and one of them had a knife, so all my tapes, all my recordings went. And these were all the songs I've written. So, I was trying to remember them all. And the joke is I'm sure the fellow who took it wouldn't know what it was, they probably chucked it away.""[51]

In 2001, during the promotion for the compilation *Wingspan*, Paul insists on the need for having to remember the songs after the robbery: "We got mugged in the street, and the studio manager said, 'You're lucky you're white, or they would have killed you.' Even though I had all my demos stolen in that robbery, I managed to remember enough of the songs to make the album."[52]

Further details about it are supplied with the re-issue of *Band on the Run*, which starts the *Paul McCartney Archive Collection* in 2010. The interviewer asks: "You were mugged when you were in Lagos. They stole tapes. Was there anything on them?" Paul replies: "Yeah, it was all of the stuff we did. It was the original demo of *Band on the Run*. It was stuff that would be worth a bit on eBay these days, you know? But no, we figured the guys who mugged us wouldn't even be remotely interested. If they'd have known, they could have just held on to them and made themselves a little fortune. But they didn't know, and we reckoned they'd probably record over them."[53]

Demos are now described as "original". A detail that adds, if it were possible, even greater mystery: by "original" does Paul mean "initial", so the ones he prepared on his own, pre-Wings rehearsals?

Last but not least. In 2024, for the 50th anniversary of *Band on the Run* and its new release, Paul states: "They took the cassettes of all the *home* demos. So that meant that I then had to remember the album."[54] It adds another little piece to this fantastic puzzle.

The narrative progression that emerges from this series of statements is interesting. It goes from general to specific details, almost with a microscopic technique. The sequence can be summed up: robbery of various equipment, including a tape recorder (1973); timing of the robbery (1973 and 1977); hint at the succession of events robbery-fainting, almost as cause-effect (1984); robbery of demo tapes (1988); need to remember the songs after the stolen demos in order to record them (1988–89); robbery of the original demos (2010), robbery of the home demos (2024).

"No problems" – Paul

A tired but happy-looking Paul McCartney flew into London's Gatwick airport in the early hours of Sunday morning after a month's recording sessions at EMI studios in Nigeria.

Accompanied by his wife Linda and Wings, guitarist Denny Laine, Paul said that "a lot of work had been covered," at the Lagos studio regarding Wings latest album. "It was a great experience and we had no problems whatsoever," added Paul.

A small group of fans gathered to welcome the McCartney party home although it was almost 4 am in the morning. Denny, looking rather more bedraggled from the plane flight which was delayed almost 10 hours said: "It's going to be the greatest Wings album yet, the atmosphere was just great."

"No movement yet on possible personnel changes or additions to the Wings line-up," says a spokesman for McCartney.

Record Mirror, 29 September 1973.

In 2017, Denny Laine offers his take: more in line with McCartney's account than with what seems to have actually happened (a classic example of the role of narrative reiteration contributing to the truth, or perhaps just a way to back Paul up), but with a further detail, probably unintentional. "Paul had his cassette of the rehearsals stolen, so we had to start from scratch."[55] Here, Denny is talking about "rehearsals", suggesting the Wings material from Scotland. Who knows?

Wings' time in Africa is also during the monsoon season, and the skies rain down red mud. Nor do the heat and humidity improve the situation. "It seemed stuffy in the studio, so I went outside for a breath of fresh air," McCartney recalls. "If anything, the air was more foul outside than in. It was then that I began to feel really terrible and had a pain across the right side of my chest and I collapsed. I could not breathe and so I collapsed and fainted."[56]

The problem is diagnosed as a bronchial spasm, since Paul is smoking like a chimney: after a couple of days of rest, things return to normal. "The doctor seemed to treat it pretty lightly and said it could be bronchial because I had been smoking too much," McCartney recalls. "But this was me in hell. I stayed in bed for a few days, thinking I was nearly dying. It was one of the most frightening periods in my life. The climate, the tensions of making a record, which had just got to succeed, and being in this totally uncivilised part of the world finally got to me ..."[57]

That experience hits Paul hard. The Nigerian adventure is proving to be tough. "There was one and a half weeks of pretty bad vibes," McCartney admits. "It felt a bit dangerous and raw and you're not sure how you're going to figure."[58]

At that point Paul decides it's time to get back home. The flight from Lagos is delayed by ten hours. When he lands in Gatwick, Paul is pictured with a big smile and says to journalists: "It was a great experience, and we had no problems whatsoever."

When not playing the part of the PR man, McCartney is less enthusiastic. "We're not sure really [what to think about it]," Paul confesses, "since the stay passed all too quickly. We had a lovely time in some ways, in what can be described as a rather strange place."[59]

But it's not the end. The album has yet to be completed and Paul chooses George Martin's AIR Studios for the final recordings. Even there, misfortune seems to hound the adventure that is *Band on the Run*.

Notes

1   Mike Reed, *McCartney on McCartney*, BBC1, 1989.

2   Chris Welch, *Onwards and Upwards, Melody Maker*, 1 December 1973.

3   Tony Clark has mentioned this to the author in many conversations over the years.

4   https://www.eltonjohn.com/stories/goodbyeyellowbrickroad-recording

5   Dermot O'Leary, Interview for ITV1, October 2010.

6   Geoff Emerick, *Here, There and Everywhere. My Life Recording the Music of The Beatles*, 2006, p. 338

7   Ginger Baker–Ginette Baker, *Ginger Baker Hellraiser*, 2009, p. 179.

8   *Homes Sweet Homes – Tina Talks to Paul McCartney, Tina*, 17 November 1973.

9   https://www.beats-onit.com/2023/10/21/
unwritten-book-of-nigerian-recording-idustry-and-talent-that-propelled-it-4/

10 Geoff Emerick, *Here, There and Everywhere. My Life Recording the Music of The Beatles*, 2006, p. 339–340.

11 John Beattie, *McCartney on the Run, Record Mirror*, p. 11, 1 December 1973.

12 Phil Hogan, *Paul McCartney: "Suddenly it just all came together", The Guardian*, 7 November 2010.

13 Geoff Emerick, *Here, There and Everywhere. My Life Recording the Music of The Beatles*, 2006, p. 339–340.

14 https://www.abbeyroad.com/news/
behind-abbey-road-studios-emi-tg12345-console-2604

15 https://producelikeapro.com/blog/the-story-of-abbey-road/

16 Geoff Emerick, *Here, There and Everywhere. My Life Recording the Music of The Beatles*, 2006, p. 339–340.

17 Keith Badman, *The Beatles. The Dream Is Over – Off the Record 2*, 2002, p. 121.

18 *You Gave Me the Answer – Celebrating 50 Years of 'Band on the Run'*, 25 January 2024, https://www.paulmccartney.com/news/
you-gave-me-the-answer-celebrating-50-years-of-band-on-the-run

19 Keith Badman, *The Beatles. The Dream Is Over – Off the Record 2*, 2002, p. 121.

20 *Band on the Run* (Deluxe Edition), *The Paul McCartney Archive Collection*, 2010, p 39.

21 All recording dates from: Allan Kozinn–Adrian Sinclair, *The McCartney Legacy. Volume 1: 1969–73*, 2022.

22 Dermot O'Leary, Interview for ITV1, October 2010.

23 Ray Telford, *Wings Fly Home Intact, Sounds*, 1 December 1973, p. 7.

24 Dermot O'Leary, Interview for ITV1, October 2010.

25 Chris Welch, *Paul McCartney. The Definitive Biography*, 1984, p. 73.

26 Billy Amendola, *Geoff Emerick: The Beatles' Studio Ground-Breaker*, *Modern Drummer*, August 2006.

27 Bill DeMain, *"I'm actually surprised we're that well-remembered. I'm just a normal musician who doesn't really think about the fame side of it"*, *Guitar World*, January 2023, https://www.guitarworld.com/features/denny-laine-paul-mccartney-and-wings.

28 Mike Reed, *McCartney on McCartney*, BBC1, 1989.

29 Andy Meek, *Denny Laine Reflects on the Tumultuous 'Gamble' of Paul McCartney & Wings' 'Band on the Run'*, *Billboard*, 2 May 2023, https://www.billboard.com/music/rock/denny-laine-paul-mccartney-band-on-the-run-wings-album-1235320301/

30 Julie Webb, *Wings in the Air*, *New Musical Express*, 27 October 1973.

31 https://www.abbeyroad.com/news/fela-ransome-kuti-and-the-africa-70-with-ginger-baker-at-abbey-road-studios-the-story-behind-the-records-with-jeff-jarratt-2773

32 https://www.abbeyroad.com/news/fela-ransome-kuti-and-the-africa-70-with-ginger-baker-at-abbey-road-studios-the-story-behind-the-records-with-jeff-jarratt-2773

33 Marc Moron *Radio interview with Paul McCartney for "WFT Podcast with Marc Maron,"* August 8, 2018.

34 *Sir Paul McCartney - Thoughts on Fela*, 10 October 2013, https://www.youtube.com/results?search_query=paul+mccartney+thoughts+on+fela

35 https://english.elpais.com/culture/2023-04-01/paul-mccartney-i-dont-know-who-you-are-when-fela-kuti-accused-the-beatle-of-cultural-appropriation.html#

36 Mark Lewisohn, *The Club Sandwich Interview*, *Club Sandwich*, no. 72, Winter 1994, p. 4.

37 *Sir Paul McCartney - Thoughts on Fela*, 10 October 2013, https://www.youtube.com/results?search_query=paul+mccartney+thoughts+on+fela

38 Allan Kozinn–Adrian Sinclair, *The McCartney Legacy. Volume 1: 1969–73*, 2022, p. 621.

39 Paul Gambaccini, *Paul McCartney in His Own Words*, 1976, p. 106.

40 Chris Welch, *Onwards and upwards*, *Melody Maker*, 1 December 1973.

41 Julie Webb, *Wings in the Air*, *New Musical Express*, 27 October 1973.

42 Julie Webb, *Wings in the Air*, *New Musical Express*, 27 October 1973.

43 John Beattie, *McCartney on the Run*, *Record Mirror*, p. 11, 1 December 1973.

44 Paul McCartney, *The Lyrics*, 2021, p. 39.

45 Chris Welch, *Onwards and upwards*, *Melody Maker*, 1 December 1973.

46 *Homes Sweet Homes, Tina Talks to Paul McCartney, Tina,* 17 November 1973.

47 *Team Spirit Brings Success to Wings, Daily Express,* 10 April 1977.

48 *The Paul McCartney Special,* home video, 1987.

49 Timothy White, *McCartney Gets Hungry Again, Musician,* February 1988.

50 Mike Reed, *Radio ATB, Club Sandwich,* no. 47–48, Spring 1988, p. 6.

51 Mike Reed, *McCartney on McCartney,* BBC1, 1989.

52 Patrick Humphries, *The Other Side of Paul McCartney,* 2001.

53 Simon Harper, *The Making of Paul McCartney – The story of Band on the Run, Clash,* 12 October 2010.

54 *Band on the Run Q&A for press,* 3 February 2024.

55 Mark Hinson, *Denny Laine talks Wings, 'Wild Life,' Linda McCartney and more, Tallahassee Democrat,* 21 September 2017, https://eu.tallahassee.com/story/entertainment/2017/09/21/ denny-laine-talks-wings-wild-life-linda-mccartney-and-more/689062001/

56 Keith Badman, *The Beatles. The Dream Is Over – Off the Record 2,* 2002, p. 112.

57 Keith Badman, *The Beatles. The Dream Is Over – Off the Record 2,* 2002, p. 112.

58 Chris Welch, *Onwards and upwards, Melody Maker,* 1 December 1973.

59 *Homes Sweet Homes – Tina Talks to Paul McCartney, Tina,* 17 November 1973.

— 4 —
AIR STUDIOS, OXFORD STREET, LONDON: GHOSTS FROM AFRICA

Oxford Circus is a major junction in London's West End, at the crossroads of Regent Street and Oxford Street, two of the busiest roads in town, crawling with activity, from shops, tourists and workers. There, in 1970, George Martin had established the first location of AIR Studios, the natural outcome of the creation of Associated Independent Recordings, the company he founded in 1965 with producers Ron Richards, John Burgess and Peter Sullivan, which aimed at changing the rules within the recording business.

Not satisfied with the fact that, as producer of all The Beatles' singles and albums created at Abbey Road up to then, he is only paid the weekly salary of a regular Parlophone employee, Martin has an idea: through this new company, he along with his business partner would finance the production costs of a record, in exchange for a royalty on sales.

Launched on 7 October 1970 through an Arabian-nights kind of ceremony, on 450 bottles of Bollinger champagne, AIR Studios initially consists of two rooms: Studio One, larger and suitable for orchestral recordings, and Studio Two, more intimate and conceived for rock bands. In the end, groups favour the bombastic drum sound guaranteed by Studio One, and shortly after comes need to open other two rooms.

Paul could experiment personally with Studio One's features in October 1972, for the recording of "Live and Let Die": an historic session, for which the big room is not enough, and some of the orchestra have to shift into the adjacent one. What happens regarding the fee received for this track confirms again to Martin how much the AIR enterprise had been a necessary if not even an essential path. When the producer starts his negotiations with Len Wood of EMI for the royalties on the single, he asks for 2%, one point less than his usual rate. But as "Live and Let Die" is a product linked to The Beatles (or at least, to one of them), George is still formally tied to his old contract dating back to 1965: 0.06 pence for each copy. And so it was: for the sales of the singles in the US (1,250,000 copies), Martin only made around £3,100.[1]

Luckily, the musical projects realised in the studios follow one another relentlessly. Over three years, AIR Studios becomes a reference point for London-based recordings, with records such as Pink Floyd's *Meddle* (1971), the Electric Light Orchestra's *ELO 2* (1972), as well as numerous film soundtracks.

Wings gather here on Tuesday 2 October to complete the Lagos recordings. Four tracks are taped from scratch over two weeks: "Jet", "Bluebird", "Nineteen Hundred and Eighty-Five", and "Oriental Nightfish", written by Linda and unreleased until 1998, when it will be issued on her posthumous record *Wide Prairie*.

At AIR Studios the technical conditions are certainly less challenging than those of EMI in Africa: not least, the studio is equipped with a 16-track machine. To assist Geoff Emerick is engineer Pete Swettenham, the ex-guitarist of Grapefruit, a band strongly intertwined with The Beatles. Their name was invented by John Lennon, and when in May 1968 the group signs a contract with Apple, the single "Lullaby" is produced by Lennon/McCartney. Although, for various reasons, this version will remain on the shelf for decades.

So, Swettenham and McCartney already know each other. When Paul meets the engineer, he soon recognises him. "I remember the first day at Studio One, I was in the control room setting up machines and Paul came in," the engineer recalls. "He just looked over me and pointed his finger to me saying, 'Peter! Grapefruit!' or something like that. So, he remembered me from back in the day."[2]

Although the first week of recordings goes smoothly, with the band laying down three tracks, even in London the enterprise of Paul, Linda and Denny seems to be marred by bad luck.

On Monday, 8 October, sessions resume with the remake of "Jet", as the first version didn't satisfy the band. During this second attempt, they realise that the tapes are starting to oxidise, due to humidity in Lagos, an issue that could have made what has been recorded useless. It's another key episode, and also in this case, it is marked by some grey areas.

Emerick remembers well what happened and he clearly apportions blame. "My assistant engineer was Pete Swettenham. He seemed competent enough, and I thought he was doing a good job, but then I started hearing something funny during the playbacks," Emerick recalls in his autobiography. "The top end on the cymbals wasn't there anymore. 'What's going on?' I asked Pete. He sidled over the multitrack machine, leaned down to have a look, and casually said, 'Well, there's a pile of oxide on the tape machine.' What?? This was a major problem, and I was furious that Pete hadn't noticed it earlier. Assistants were supposed to keep the heads of the tape machine scrupulously clean, and they were supposed to stay on top of things like this."[3]

But Swettenham does not agree. And his explanation has a specific professional reason. "It's a bit unfair, because it didn't really happen that way," he clarifies. "On 'Jet' Geoff noticed that the drums started sounding a bit 'wooden'. When in his book he says I should have noticed that, I think it's because his training at EMI was a lot different. What they do is that is that the engineer seat in different room than the assistant and they use an intercom. At AIR, the assistant would seat next to the engineer and has a remote control for starting and stopping the tape. So that's why I didn't notice it, visually." [4]

Once Emerick understands what's going on, he has to make a quick decision. Stop everything and warn McCartney of what's happening, or try to find an acceptable technical solution? "When Geoff noticed that the sound was going off a bit," Swettenham again remembers, "he took a look, and we could see that there was oxide coming off the tape. He didn't say anything to Paul and moved on. But I think the sound of the snare on Jet may have contributed to its popularity! It's very sort of boxy!" [5]

It's a serious problem, but Emerick manages to keep his *sangfroid*. "Not only was it irreversible, each time you played back or even rewound the tape, it got worse," Emerick recalls. "The only thing you could do was to quickly make a second-generation copy of the audio on a good reel of tape and hope that the sound hadn't deteriorated too badly by that point. It was just our luck to have this one bad reel of tape just as we were recording such a great song." [6]

It's a delicate moment, another episode that goes down to shape the myth of the *Band on the Run* recordings. According to Emerick, the reason for everything not being lost is due precisely to the choice of tapes by the record company: "We used EMI Tape I think it was coded 77," Emerick says. "The classical engineers were beginning to like AGFA I can't remember the # but they liked it because of the enhanced top end, the American brands were not used in EMI Studios. One great thing about the EMI Tape was that the backing of the tape never disintegrated so as far as I know to this day the oxide does not shed from the backing. I think it was due to the whale product in the makeup. I guess working in other studios it would probably have been Scotch tape." [7]

Luckily, a ray of light radiates in the studio that same day. He's Remi Kabaka, a session man born in Ghana but who grew up in Nigeria and has been a resident in London for quite some time (he was also part of Ginger Baker's Air Force), who contributes percussion on "Bluebird".

During the sessions Swettenham can see with his own eyes the experience and the skills both of McCartney and Emerick: "I witnessed Paul playing drums, and he's a very good drummer," Swettenham says. "They also recorded the backing vocals all together. They don't resonate the same way if you don't do them together. Geoff's got a particular technique for miking the drums, which seems to be not perfect until you blend it all with the rest of the instruments. Thanks to his ear."[8]

After the completion of the new tracks and the overdubbing of instruments and vocals on the Lagos material, the sessions stop for the weekend of 13 and 14 October. On that Sunday, Emerick and Swettenham prepare a rough mix of the album.

* * *

Paul, on the other hand, carries on the work at home. The orchestral overdubbing on some of the album tracks is set for Wednesday, 17 October. McCartney gets in touch with Tony Visconti, who was at his peak as a producer for glam rock stars such as Marc Bolan and David Bowie, asking him to prepare string, brass and woodwind arrangements and scores for some of the tracks.

Visconti, who is married to Welsh singer Mary Hopkin, who Paul knows from the Apple days – her single "Those Were the Days" was released along with "Hey Jude" and others in 1968 for the launch of the new Beatles' label and Paul had written "Goodbye" for her in 1969 – goes to Cavendish Avenue to better understand the work that has to be done.

The atmosphere is relaxed, with Linda and Mary Hopkin sitting on the sofa, sipping tea and chatting. "Paul said, 'I like you to write some string arrangement.' I knew him through Mary Hopkin, who was my wife at the time. He asked me to go to his house in St. John's Wood, it was on a Sunday," the producer recalls vividly. "We sat in the big living room, and Paul and I sat at the piano, and he started playing the songs to me. Sometimes on piano, sometimes from a rough mix. He likes to just dictate parts, whistling a part or playing the top part on the piano."[9]

In fact, Paul has clear ideas about those parts: early recordings and mixes from the Lagos and AIR Studios tapes show, for example, McCartney singing the woodwind part on "Picasso's Last Words" and the closing sax line on "Jet", note for note. Nonetheless, Visconti soon realises that there's something strange and forming an idea of the songs was quite difficult. "He only played snippets of the songs that he wanted me to write on, he was terrified that these would be bootlegged! I only heard the beginning of 'Band on the Run' and the section where horns were supposed to be, then he stopped the tape. I couldn't hear the rest! Also, for 'Picasso's Last Words', I've heard just the bits he wanted me to orchestrate not the whole song … 'Bluebird', just the bit where he wanted the sax. It was seven songs in all."[10]

At least, the producer has a gut feeling that he's going to be part of something extraordinary. "My impression of what I did hear was that this was going to be an incredible album,"[11] Visconti adds.

The best is yet to come: "I was thrilled to be doing this for one of my idols," Visconti says. "But not so thrilled when he told me he needed all arrangements [in three days]!" [12]

The big day is 17 October, and it's a long-drawn out session. Seven tracks are overdubbed with orchestra (a 60-piece ensemble called the Beaux Arts Orchestra) or woodwind and brass: "Band on the Run", "Jet", "Picasso's Last Words", "Nineteen Hundred and Eighty-Five" – these four with the full orchestra, the addition of a sax quartet on "Jet" and clarinet and bassoon on "Picasso's Last Words" – "No Words" (with a lighter string quartet), and "Bluebird" and "Mrs. Vandebilt" both enriched with sax solos. "I showed up in the studio about ten o'clock in the morning, and I had great bags under my eyes," Visconti recalls. "I conducted the orchestra for eight hours, and Paul was just full of praise and admiration for me." [13]

What happened to the tapes on which Emerick had to intervene also has an impact on the orchestral overdubs: "Because of the humidity in Nigeria, the oxide fell off the tape," Visconti remembers. "Geoff Emerick had to restore the condition of the tape by copying it into sixteen tracks and putting heavy compression on each channel so you wouldn't hear the dropouts. That gave us only eight more tracks to do all the orchestral stuff and the backing vocals. It's super compressed … But that made a kind of a sound that started a trend." [14]

Among the musicians hired by Visconti is Howie Casey, an old acquaintance of Paul since the Hamburg days and ex-leader of the Liverpool band Howie Casey and the Seniors. He plays the two sax solos, on "Bluebird" and "Mrs. Vandebilt".

Casey also takes part in the horn section on "Jet". Alongside him are Dave Coxhill, Jeff Daly and Phil Kenzie, a session man from Liverpool who did an overdub on "Let It Be" in 1970 and who has also played with Harrison and Lennon. The instructions for the recording surprise him, to say the least: "I was to pull in an enormous number of saxophones as far as I was concerned," Kenzie says. "'My God, how many do you want?' I had to get two baritone players, three tenor players, two alto players. This was one Hell of a sax section. I walk in there and there's two more there. One of which was another tenor player making us four in all. He was a friend of mine from Liverpool called Howie Casey. He was one of the first to recommend The Beatles to go to Germany as it were." [15]

Clearly, the shortage of time given to Visconti for hiring musicians has a certain impact in the studio. When it comes to assigning the parts, there's a bit of confusion. "One of the baritone players was borrowing my baritone to play," Kenzie also recalls. "He was actually an alto player. They had phoned the union and found a guy who played bass sax. I didn't know him at all because I didn't book him. … It's the only session where I've ever played with a bass sax on it. You can hear the power in the beginning of that song."[16]

Notwithstanding Visconti's phenomenal contribution, the credit for his work seems to cause some issues over the years. At first, everything seems great: "Paul came to my house a couple of weeks later to play me the final mixes," Visconti reveals. "And really wanted to know my opinion, and if there was anything I could add to it."[17]

But when *Band on the Run* is released, only a "special thanks" to him is mentioned on the back cover, not specifying the arrangement work. "I like to call the '70s the 'I did it my way' generation," Visconti would later comment. "The Rolling Stones had great producers, but they never gave them credit. I think it was to create the illusion that 'it's just us, we go in the studio, take our capes off, make music and then we leave.' Nowadays you see the Grammys, someone gets up and credits everyone – 'I'd like to thank my team and God and Jesus.'"[18]

For the 2010 reissue of the album, McCartney carefully reconsiders, and Visconti is credited with a comment from Paul: "You've got your credit back!". But when, in early 2024, the 50th Anniversary Edition of *Band on the Run* is issued, using the original sleeve, the credit disappeared again. Irritated, Visconti feels compelled to comment on Twitter: "I play no small part in it as the orchestrator of all the orchestral parts. I didn't get a credit on its first release, but I did get my credit on its 25th Anniversary release. Now, with its 50th Anniversary release, I am again not credited. Go figure!"

* * *

The last *coup de théâtre* is for the mixing of the album. The time is up. Emerick has other engagements and a diplomatic effort by all the parties involved is needed to end the work. "We went back to London and finished it off; I was due to do another album, I think the band was called Triumvirate with Gerry Bron," Emerick recalls. "My manager at that time John Burgess said to him, 'Look, Geoff's come back, and [Paul] wants a few more days. Can you give up three of your days so he can mix *Band on the Run*?' and Gerry said 'No'. At that time Paul was going to kidnap me. Paul said, I'm going to kidnapping you, Geoff. Eventually I actually mixed the album in three days at a studio called Kingsway in London."[19] In truth, the three days at Kingsway are not enough, and at the eleventh hour, the team move to Abbey Road to finish the mixing. The engineer works intensely and with care, trying to capture all the sonic characteristics that would make this album so important, notwithstanding the adversities encountered.

And so, in a rush, with the following session already looming, Emerick completes yet another record that would make history.

Notes

1   Kenneth Womack, *Sound Pictures. The Life of Beatles Producer George Martin. The Later Years 1966–2016*, 2018, p. 385.

2   Author's interview with Pete Swettenham, 27 October 2014.

3   Geoff Emerick, *Here, There and Everywhere. My Life Recording the Music of The Beatles*, 2006, p. 351.

4   Author's interview with Pete Swettenham, 27 October 2014.

5   Author's interview with Pete Swettenham, 27 October 2014.

6   Geoff Emerick, *Here, There and Everywhere. My Life Recording the Music of The Beatles*, 2006, p. 351.

7   https://gearspace.com/board/interviews/1374843-interview-geoff-emerick.html

8   Author's interview with Pete Swettenham, 27 October 2014.

9   https://www.youtube.com/watch?v=EIwW705Lr_s

10 https://www.youtube.com/watch?v=EIwW705Lr_s

11 Will Hodgkinson, *"You'd do anything for a Beatle…" Tony Visconti On Working With Paul McCartney*, Mojo, 8 February 2024, https://www.mojo4music.com/articles/stories/tony-visconti-on-working-with-paul-mccartney/.

12 Tony Visconti, *Bowie, Bolan and The Brooklyn Boy*, 2007, p. 204.

13 John Tobler–Stuart Grundy, *The Record Producers*, 1982, p. 181.

14 https://www.youtube.com/watch?v=EIwW705Lr_s

15 Robert von Bernewitz, https://musicguy247.typepad.com/my-blog/2015/02/phil-kenzie-interview.html.

16 Robert von Bernewitz, https://musicguy247.typepad.com/my-blog/2015/02/phil-kenzie-interview.html.

17 John Tobler–Stuart Grundy, *The Record Producers*, 1982, p. 181.

18 Andrew Goldman, *Tony Visconti Will Lie for David Bowie*, The New York Times Magazine, 29 March 2013, https://www.nytimes.com/2013/03/31/magazine/tony-visconti-will-lie-for-david-bowie.html

19 Greg Schmidt, *The Victor Company | Geoff Emerick (EMI/HMV/Beatles) | His Master's Voice: Music Industry Interviews*, 18 January 2023, https://www.youtube.com/watch?v=C6czTmxnH_4.

— 5 —
"DOWN TO LIVERPOOL WHERE THEY PLAY THE WEST COAST SOUND" (THE SINGLE "HELEN WHEELS")

T he discography of *Band on the Run*, or at least the discography relating to the material from these sessions, starts on 19 October 1973, when the single "Helen Wheels", one of the tracks recorded in Africa by the Paul–Linda–Denny Laine trio, appears on the UK market.

Four months have already passed since the previous McCartney record, "Live and Let Die". When, in early October, Wings gather at AIR Studios in London, this track is ready and Emerick soon prepares a mix. With the Christmas season impending and the album still to be finished, there's no time to lose. For some reason, Paul thinks that "Helen Wheels" has a certain commercial appeal, notwithstanding its simplicity.

It marks McCartney's return to rock'n'roll, and the proposal of a straightforward song – as opposed to the magniloquence of "Live and Let Die" – confirms that Paul was always attuned to the diversity of his musical output; this ability would reveal itself to be one of the keys to his relentless commercial success in the Seventies.

If on the one hand McCartney was interested in the record market, on the other he couldn't ignore its rules and conventions, regardless of his intellectual honesty. And "Helen Wheels" is best known for being at the centre of a marketing strategy. Following a golden rule always applied by The Beatles, Paul avoided including a previously released standalone single on an album: McCartney himself had continued this tradition when he left "Another Day" off *RAM*. Later on, this habit would cause him a few headaches: the examples of "Mull of Kintyre" (not on *London Town* in 1978) and "Goodnight Tonight" (which Paul refused to include on *Back to the Egg*, 1979) would create friction with his record company.

This time, however, Paul had to yield to Capitol's insistence: "The companies would like a single on the album. It makes more sense merchandising wise," McCartney would comment later. "But sometimes, I just have to remember that this isn't a record retail store I'm running; this is supposed to be some kind of art. And if it doesn't fit in, it doesn't fit in. They're not really strict on it. We've got a lot of artistic control, thank goodness. But I can see the wisdom of what they're asking. I remember Al Coury – we weren't gonna put 'Helen Wheels' on the American *Band on the Run,* and he rang up and said, 'I can give you quarter of a million more sales if you put it on.' And I said, 'We don't want it, we really don't want it.' I was being kind of reticent, and in the end, he persuaded me anyway. He said, 'Just do it, just in America or something.'"[1]

The release of "Helen Wheels" comes shortly before that of *Band on the Run.* The time between the release of single and of the LP was really too tight to indicate to the public that the track would not be part of the new album, with the risk of disappointing them and thus compromising sales.

Capitol's marketing department puts pressure on McCartney to include the track on the American edition of the album: it would make the LP more appealing in commercial terms, even though Paul had decided not to put any singles on it. In the end, McCartney accepts through gritted teeth: thus, *Band on the Run* becomes the only one of McCartney's studio albums to feature different track listings on the UK and US editions.

❊   ❊   ❊

Helen Wheels

(Paul and Linda McCartney)

Recording: 7 September 1973 **Location:** EMI Studios, Apapa

"**H**elen Wheels" proves, once again, McCartney's ability to turn any aspect of his life into music. The inspiration came from Helen Wheels, the affectionate nickname Paul had given to his Land Rover, the means of transport that drove him, Linda (and, occasionally, Wings) from his farm in Scotland to London and back. Another symbol of freedom. Paul: "It's a name we gave to our Land Rover, which is a trusted vehicle that gets us around Scotland … Liverpool is on the West coast of England, so that is all that means."[2]

For Paul it's both a geographical and lexical challenge. "That song described a trip down the M6, which is the big motorway to get from Scotland down south to England," McCartney says. "So that song was my attempt to try and put England on the map. All the Chuck Berry songs you ever heard always had things like 'Birmingham, Alabama!' shouted out, these American places like

'Tallahassee!' But you couldn't put the English ones in. It always sounded daft to us. 'Scunthorpe!' 'Warrington!' It doesn't sound as funky."[3]

The title could be a wordplay on "Hell on Wheels" (sung in the chorus), which was originally the itinerant collection of gambling houses, saloons and brothels that followed the army of Union Pacific railroad workers in America in 1860s, but now means something (or someone) that is extremely problematic.

Recorded in Lagos at the end of the first week of the sessions, "Helen Wheels" proves more complicated than planned, notwithstanding its simple structure and style, a boogie almost completely on one chord. The track is committed to tape rather quickly, although, to tell the truth, a couple of tricks have to be devised to put it down without going overboard. Not surprisingly, the tape compiled by Emerick and containing the Lagos recordings features a soon-aborted take that precedes the master.

In fact, the drum tempo turns out to be hard for McCartney. Thus, Linda offers her contribution by counting the beats (she can be heard toward the end, from 3:05 until the fade out, shouting "one, two, three, four") and keeping the time on cowbell, while Paul had to come up with something else. "The only one I couldn't get behind was 'Helen Wheels' because it's a shuffle and I find them extremely hard to play," McCartney says. "We just had to break down the drum part in that one and I played shuffle on cymbal and Denny whacked the bass drum for me."[4]

Closer inspection reveals a rather crowded rhythm part, with many drum rolls and an almost continuous use of cymbals, different to the other the *Band on the Run* songs, where these are practically absent. The rest of the arrangement sees Laine on rhythm guitar and Linda on Minimoog, while Paul plays walking bass and the guitar solos: a raw contribution, all played with fast licks, that reinforce the whole track. McCartney's vocal part is almost mechanical, with well-crafted response backing vocals.

The result is a hypnotic boogie all in the key of A (the only chord change is at the end of the chorus, when the song resolves to E and then to A minor), in a surprisingly unpolished arrangement. "Helen Wheels" is a galloping road-song in the same vein as songs such as "On the Road Again" by Canned Heat.

But there's no room for the long and dusty American roads. It lists instead the main towns along the M6 from Scotland down towards London: Glasgow, Carlisle, Kendal, Liverpool and Birmingham. "It's got a lot of memories for me, that Land Rover with everything in the back, dogs, kids," Paul recalls. "Us all up at the front, and me, driving on this epic journey!"[5]

The lyrics also include a little cross reference: "With 'Sailor Sam' I was initially just wanting a rhyme for Birmingham," McCartney explains. "And then I thought, 'Wait a minute: Sailor Sam's on 'Band on the Run.' He makes a little guest appearance here, as a cameo in a film."[6] A connection that would help to justify its inclusion in the US version of the album.

> **Musicians:**
>
> **Paul McCartney** vocals, backing vocals, bass, electric guitar, drums • **Linda McCartney** backing vocals, cow bell, Minimoog • **Denny Laine** backing vocals, electric guitar, drums

* * *

Credited to "Paul McCartney and Wings" and released on 19 October 1973 in the UK and 5 November in America, "Helen Wheels" is issued in a plain sleeve, with the Apple logo on the label. A video is also shot; it alternates images of Paul, Linda and Denny Laine while driving a cabriolet and other vehicles with the three miming their instrumental performances in a studio. A curious detail: in the original film, Linda wears a jacket with an animal fur collar, which would be disguised using computer processing for inclusion in the video *The Paul McCartney Special* in 1986. Only around 1975 did the McCartneys decide to become vegetarians.

Apart from the US, commercially speaking the single is only a relatively minor hit in a number of other countries. However, it makes no. 12 in the UK and the Top 10 in Canada, where it peaks at no. 4. "Helen Wheels" is certainly less original and imaginative in comparison to "Live and Let Die", but critics warm to this stylistic upheaval. NME title their review "Cracka from Macca", noting that the track features "cranking, tubular-metal Canned Heat style guitar".

Richard Green writes in the *Record Mirror*: "McCartney the truck drivin' man. After a string of soppy ballads and the heavy production job on 'Live and Let Die,' Paul, with his amputated Wings (Paul, Linda and Denny Laine) have remembered their rockin' roots."

If "Helen Wheels" confirms McCartney's talent to produce hits blending his own characteristic style with the current sounds and fashions, his definitive post-Beatles offering is just around the corner. *Band on the Run* would confirm him as one of the major acts of the Seventies' pop and rock scene. The record would mark the pinnacle of McCartney's commercial success and his full rehabilitation in the eyes of the critics, validating his poetic skills alongside those of a hit-maker.

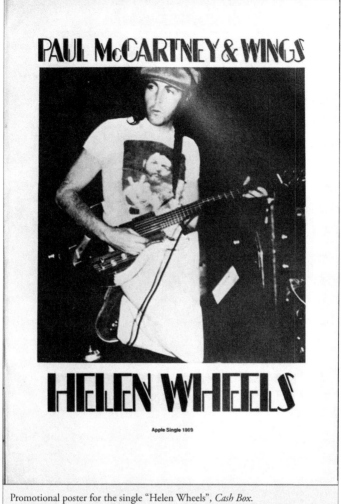

Promotional poster for the single "Helen Wheels", *Cash Box*.

Notes

1   Paul Gambaccini, *Paul McCartney, Rolling Stone*, 30 March 1979.

2   Paul Gambaccini, *Paul McCartney in His Own Words*, 1976, p. 83.

3   Timothy White, *McCartney Gets Hungry Again, Musician*, February 1988.

4   John Beatties, *McCartney on the Run, Record Mirror*, 1 December 1973.

5   Paul McCartney, *The Lyrics*, 2021, p. 260.

6   Paul McCartney, *The Lyrics*, 2021, p. 260.

— 6 —
BAND ON THE RUN:
THE ALBUM

*B*and on the Run carries with it an incredible story, and it's undeniable that the album represents a watershed within McCartney's post-Beatles career. The exuberance of the songs, the craft of the arrangements, a certain common thread within the lyrics, which principally deal with the subject of freedom and so almost help to create a concept album, make it a milestone of Seventies' rock.

The impact that has on McCartney's post-Beatles career, both in terms of critical acclaim and commercial success, is noteworthy. The album not only marks a complete reconciliation between Paul and the critics, but overall, *Band on the Run* quickly earns the reputation of being McCartney's pop art masterpiece. Paul's fame and popularity as a solo artist or with Wings would be irrevocably tied to this record over the decades.

On its release, the reaction of the musical press is almost one of relief: in its entirety *Band on the Run* is considered a fine album. Taken at face value, the album is indeed a collection of catchy tunes, arranged in the best pop tradition: in sum it is quintessential McCartney, a quality that – in an opinion shared by many critics and fans – has been seen only sporadically on his previous records. This is an ungenerous assessment of McCartney's production up to then, which in *RAM* had probably found its most imaginative and brilliant episode, even though this is often overlooked by the critics. And yet it cannot be denied that Paul's image as a musician was linked to commercial pop, to catchy and refined melodies, more than to experimental and eccentric productions.

Which is why, at the time of its release, *Band on the Run* has both audience and critics agreeing on the qualities of the LP, maybe even a little more than it merits. The record's main quality is cohesion: it isn't a simple combination of excellent pop songs and musical ideas. The fact that the album also features inspired lyrics – both simple and poetic – which principally deal with the subject of freedom, is a triumphant accomplishment: for its influence on popular culture, *Band on the Run* still remains the only McCartney solo production that stands comparison – albeit relatively distantly – with the output of The Beatles.

One of the most intriguing aspects of the record is, in fact, the lyrical one. Not as much for the complexity of its rhymes – but rather for a certain consistency of themes.

The subject of freedom is indeed explored practically everywhere on side one of the album, although it seems less evident on side two. But wait: isn't there also freedom on "Mamunia", a word of African origin which sounds like nonsense to a Western audience? Isn't it freedom to surrender yourself to the memories of a lost love, as "No Words" seems to tell? Isn't it freedom in a track such as "Picasso's Last Words", assembled aspiring to the cubist style of the most important contemporary artist, made of fragmentation and reconstruction, in spite of the most typical structures of popular music? Or imagining a year like in "1985", where "no one's ever left alive"?

And so, more than an anthology of freedom, just one kind of freedom, *Band on the Run* is an anthology of freedoms, plural. Because each one of us has our own freedom, our own chains to break, and a flight to be made.

* * *

From both a technical and musical point of view, *Band on the Run* is an album still to be analysed in depth. Based on analysis of the tracks and some of Linda's Polaroids included in the album's original booklet, other pictures appearing in the book *Wingspan*, in the book accompanying the *Band on the Run* Deluxe Edition and lately with the 50th Anniversary Edition of the album, we can reconstruct, at least in part, the instrumentation employed during the sessions in Lagos and at AIR Studios in London.

Paul McCartney:

1970 Fender Jazz bass: Although Paul at this point was almost exclusively employing his Rickenbacker (which is featured in all photos and images from the sessions of *McCartney, RAM, Wild Life* and *Red Rose Speedway*), according to the pictures from Lagos there's no trace of the instrument. An oversight? A deliberate choice, maybe not add further weight to equipment for the trip? Or better to leave the instrument safely at home, instead of taking it on the trip, thus exposing it to the possibility of what happened to the Höfner some months before? Or, last but not least, Paul is planning not to record his parts in Africa, but to overdub them later?

The fact is that McCartney plays a Fender Jazz instead, and, moreover, one owned by Denny Laine! Let's look closely to the photos taken in the Lagos studio, in which Paul holds the instrument: being left-handed, he has to keep it upside down. The logo is shown bottom up.

Not only does Paul seem to be at ease playing it, but we also know that he will do so again: a couple of years later, during the taping of "Listen to What the Man Said" in New Orleans, where Wings were recording the *Venus and Mars* album, McCartney is again seen playing Laine's Fender Jazz.

Fender Mustang bass: in another photo, McCartney holds this model, again owned by Denny Laine. We don't know if it has been actually played or if Paul is just posing.

Rickenbacker bass: in a photo in a promotional video for the 50th Anniversary Edition of *Band on the Run* McCartney is portrayed playing this bass at London's AIR Studios. The instrument is employed on the three tracks recorded from scratch ("Jet", "Bluebird" and "Nineteen Hundred and Eighty-Five") or when Paul decides the replace the original part ("Let Me Roll It").

1967 Martin D-28 acoustic guitar: this is the guitar that Paul still uses today, both in the studio and in his concerts. It's probably his favourite.

1971 Martin D12-28 12-string acoustic guitar: rarely played by McCartney, it's probably heard on "Picasso's Last Words".

1970 Ludwig Standard S-330 drums: a kit Paul built himself and used for the recording of his first solo album *McCartney*.

1962 Epiphone Casino electric guitar: judging from the sound, it could be the one used for the solo and riffs on the title track "Band on the Run".

1970 Ampeg Dan Armstrong Plexi electric guitar: its main feature is a transparent body. Famous for being used in 1981–1982 in a photo session by Clive Arrowsmith.

1971 Fender Rhodes Suitcase electric piano: Fender Rhodes parts are heard on "Band on the Run" and "Mrs. Vandebilt".

1971 Fender Rhodes Mark I Stage electric piano: this could be the electric piano heard on "Picasso's Last Words".

Hamburg Steinway baby grand piano: used at AIR Studios. Piano parts are on "Nineteen Hundred and Eight-Five", "Jet" and "Band on the Run".

Linda McCartney:

1970 Minimoog Model D synthesizer

Denny Laine:

1970s Fender Telecaster Hollowbody electric guitar

1970s **Martin 00-18 acoustic guitar**

1960s **Gibson J-200 acoustic guitar:** probably employed on "Picasso's Last Words".

* * *

One subject to be discussed is whether *Band on the Run* is a Paul McCartney album. Or by Paul McCartney & Wings, to which is attributed (although the initial release of the album by Capitol in the US shows only "Paul McCartney" on the spine)? Or by Wings? The role of Denny Laine is considered crucial by many, not only for his instrumental contribution, but overall, for being loyal to Paul and for representing a sort of human glue within the trio. At first, anyway, he seems quite disenchanted about it. "I'm kind of an odd job man in this group," Laine admits, maybe with a touch of bitterness. "I look at *Band on the Run* as definitely 'their' album. We're not a group anymore, I'm one of the three or I'm an individual. If it was Wings, I'd feel more a part of it. But it's not my songs, and I like to feel more involved, and contribute as much as they do."[1]

Denny seems conscious of the situation and does not hide a certain embarrassment. "I'm game for anything," he suggests, "but it's down to waiting for him to suggest it, it's not up to me. If I were to suggest it, it probably wouldn't cut any ice even though I practically live with them all the time. I can't get over that he's who he is."[2]

* * *

Band on the Run

(Paul and Linda McCartney)

> **Recording:** 3–7 September 1973 (basic track and overdubs part I), 3–10 October 1973 (overdubs part II) and 17 October 1973 (overdubs part III) **Location:** EMI Studios, Apapa (basic track and overdubs part I) and AIR Studios, London (overdubs parts II–III)

This epic track opens *Band on the Run*, setting the tone for the record and its conceptual and sonic frame. The themes of freedom, redemption and escape from constraints and toward a better future could not find a more fitting portrayal.

Many references are contained in the song. The first deals with social redemption. "At the time bands like us and the Eagles were feeling like and being treated like outlaws and desperados," Paul says, recalling his experiences with drugs busts from 1972. "I mean, people were getting busted for pot, that is. And our argument was that we didn't want to be outlaws. We wanted to … make our music and live in peace. And that's what the song was about; it was my reaction to the whole scene … It was during the era when everyone was like desperados, people were getting busted left, right and centre of things, so the spirit was like 'We're all in this together'. So, anything about desperados or 'on the run' kind of united people against the authority. And, you know, we happened to be part of that. So, I got this idea of 'Band on the Run'."[3]

A real episode from 12 February 1972 during the *Wings' University Tour* could be behind it. Seiwell: "I think at one of those places that we stayed; Paul had a little beef with the owner over something. And somehow or another, his elbow kind of hit the guy in the face. Don't think he did it intentionally, but all of a sudden, his oldest girl [Heather] is running around saying, 'Everybody get up, pack up. We got to get out of here. The cops are coming'. And it was hilarious, but I really think that that's where he got the term 'band on the run' from."[4]

A second subject, much more material but equally important, is tied to the financial and artistic emancipation that The Beatles were craving, freeing themselves from their business issues. In fact, the song includes a remark made by Harrison at Apple in the Spring of 1973. "It started off with 'If I ever get out of here.' That came from a remark George made at one of the Apple meetings," Paul says. "He was saying that we were all prisoners in some way, some kind of remark like that. 'If we ever get out of here,' the prison bit, and I thought that would be a nice way to start an album."[5]

Born therefore out of different moments, "Band on the Run" is a cut-and-paste job in the best McCartney tradition, and stitches together three sections. Musically, an almost a progressive version of Wings, in a striking narrative succession, where the lyrics find a wonderful counterpart in the different musical moments, each one with its style. Also, from a harmonic point of view, the song is worth being analysed for its chord choices and its key and tempo changes.

Phase one: the calm resignation of the prisoners. This first part serves as an introduction (to the track and to the whole album), with the wiry-sounding guitars and Minimoog balanced by a calm rhythmic accompaniment. The opening riff (until 0:37) is a very characteristic phrase and proves that simplicity more than technical skills is the main ingredient to create memorable musical parts: backed by Fender Rhodes, the guitar practically shifts all in double stops, principally hitting the top two strings! Ingeniously, McCartney employs Dmaj7 and G/Gm chords throughout this section: a clever trick, which creates a mellow and suspended background that perfectly expresses the mood of the characters, forced into detention and halfway between a lethargic state and the anxiety boiling underneath. Paul's vocal is accompanied by those of Linda and Denny,

The Fender Rhodes Suitcase electric piano used during the Lagos sessions.

creating very tight and precise three-part harmonies, with the effective use of glissandos and crescendos. The lyric, with its hypnotic vocals, depicts the moral and physical fatigue of the imprisoned, locked in jail and with no hope for their future.

Phase two, the tension mounts … What if we try to get out? This second segment starts at 1:19: it's aggressive, with heavily distorted, syncopated, and irregular guitars. Electric piano also is present. A solo guitar part, somewhat buried in the mix, wails on the background, The tone is raging and replaces desperation with a rebel yell, which glimpses a possibility of redemption, in its repetitive chant of "If I ever get out of here". Paul, Linda and Denny sing in harmony for this choral part, with Linda even adding a fourth, short vocal to the last "here", in a very low register.[6] The guitar sound in these two sections is characterised by oversaturation, an issue probably connected to the oxidisation of the album tapes.

In this section and in the previous one, Linda plays two simple and yet ingenious Minimoog parts, both creating a sonic counterbalance: during the intro, a phrase with two notes alternating in quick succession, in the rocking part contrasting the wail of the guitars with long sustained notes. This part shifts to the key of Am, alternating only D and Am chords. Again, a very simple backdrop to address the anger that starts to break out and that precedes the action.

Phase three: the escape. At 2:06 a majestic orchestral climax introduces the third section – opening with some shiny acoustic guitar strummed chords, with a change of key from D to C – expressing the sense of freedom of the fugitives. The recording of the orchestra, entrusted to Tony Visconti, proves to be rather problematic, notwithstanding its brevity. "I was asked to orchestrate that little interlude between the slow part of 'Band on the Run' and the fast part," Visconti says. "And there's no rhythmical relationship between the two tempos … I remember taking a long time to conduct all of the 50 musicians to play that little phrase … It was only five bars long, but it took ages to get right in synch with the track."[7] Two repeated phrases, which double note for note the work of McCartney and Laine's guitar in the basic track, buried by this monumental contribution.

The three minutes that follow are pure McCartney pop: with its ebullient vocal and its catchy chorus, this part is packed with guitar riffs and features an excellent drum performance that caused worthy praise to be bestowed on Paul. He also contributes a small piano part: it's deeply buried in the mix between 4:40 and 4:42.

A burst of enthusiasm. The structure having different sections and the nature of the plot make it a somewhat cinematic song. "Certain aspects of it remind me of Butch Cassidy and the Sundance Kid," McCartney says. "The undertaker is ringing a bell because he's upset, he has so few customers. Sailor Sam's a character out of Rupert Bear, the comic strip by Mary Tourtel."[8] The harmony includes both C and F chords in their major 7th variations, thus creating a hopeful mood: maybe it's not coincidental that it's also a major 7th chord that opens the first section. Also noteworthy is the use of some bars in three-four time throughout this section.

McCartney accompanies the track with a brilliant and sharp drum performance. In the first section, Paul only employs rimshots, in the second he adds hi hat and some handclaps reinforce the rhythm. In the third part, we can note a very limited use of cymbals, but on the other hand drum roll and toms in counterpoint are in evidence. It's impossible to say, in the absence of any proof, whether McCartney's part is redolent of that of Seiwell from the Scotland rehearsals. The drummer seems to recall it that way: "Paul didn't change much of what we played

The 1970 Fender Jazz.

when he recorded it," Denny says. "I thought the two-track demo we made was better than the final record, to tell you the truth."[9]

Anyway, no drum part is protected by copyright; for sure, this is the most distinctive performance of the whole album. Someone noteworthy notices it: "Actually, the greatest compliment for that was when, a year after or so, I went out to visit John in Los Angeles [end of March 1974], and Keith Moon was staying with him," Paul recalls. "And Keith said, 'Man, but who's doing the drumming on that album? I really like it!'"[10]

The key is the volume of the instrument, kept high in the mix. A deliberate choice by Emerick: "Musically wise, the main focal point of that album is the drum sound and I never tried to lose the drum sound," the engineer explains. "Everything was complementary to the drums on that. The drums are really loud and sort of carry the whole thing."[11]

The bass part is unmistakably McCartney. He plays in counterpoint in the first section, with a little riff featuring fast and close notes, makes an assault in the second segment and gallops away in the third part. With its slightly flattened tuning, in the latter portion the bass has an exuberant quality.

So "Band on the Run" traces the path to a powerful work in artistic terms. It's only the start to an incredible journey.

Musicians:

Paul McCartney vocals, backing vocals, electric guitar, electric piano, piano, bass, drums • **Linda McCartney** backing vocals, Minimoog • **Denny Laine** backing vocals, acoustic and electric guitar • **Beaux Arts Orchestra** full orchestra

* * *

Jet

(Paul and Linda McCartney)

Recording: 9 October 1973 (basic track) and 17 October 1973 (overdubs)
Location: AIR Studios, London

Although there is no doubt about the inspiration behind this song, in particular behind its title, over the course of the decades Paul has changed his story many times about "Jet".

Let's clear the field of misunderstandings. "Jet" is inspired by a dog. Who's Jet? He's a Labrador puppy, owned by McCartney. Funnily enough, it's the third McCartney song whose title contains the name of a dog, after "Martha My Dear" (with the name of his sheepdog and released in 1968 on *The Beatles*) and "There You Go, Eddie", which cites the name of his Yorkshire Terrier, Eddie, which was rehearsed in 1969 during the *Get Back* sessions but is unreleased to date.

The story of "Jet" is quite lovely. "We've got a Labrador puppy who is a runt, the runt of a litter," Paul recalls. "We bought her along a roadside in a little pet shop, out in the country one day. She was a bit of a wild dog, a wild girl who wouldn't stay in. We have a big wall around our house in London, and she wouldn't stay in, she always used to jump the wall. She'd go out on the town for the evening, like Lady and the Tramp. She came back one day pregnant. She proceeded to walk into the garage and have this litter. Seven perfect little black Labradors, and she's not black, she's tan. So, we worked out it must have been a black Labrador. So 'Jet' was one of the puppies."[12]

Paul has written the song in 1973, while in Scotland. "I'd gone off on my own to get away from everything and there I was sitting in the middle of a field when the song came bounding up. The puppy's name gave me a spark of an idea, and out came this song about a girl called Jet."[13] Thus, Jet seems to be the name of a female character.

There's an interesting piece that helps us place the composition of the tune around Spring or early Summer of that year. In the August 1973 newsletter of Wings Fun Club, compiled by MPL employee Nicky, is the following: "Poppy, Paul's Labrador, had 7 puppies about 2 months ago. Paul and Linda besides having Poppy and the puppies, have a dalmatian – given to Paul last year for his birthday, called Lucky, Poppy's puppy, Captain Midnight and the famed old English sheepdog – Martha."[14]

In 2010, Paul offers another version of the story. Being the most recent, it's taken as true by many. "It was named after a pony, "Paul says. "We had a little pony for the kids, in Scotland and it was called Jet." [15] This option finds further confirmation. Laine: "Actually it was written about one of the horses up in Scotland. [The lyric] 'With a wind in your hair of a thousand laces" … This is a horse! It has to do with travel."[16] But the pony was acquired around 1975, so it's likely that he was named after the title of the song more than the other way around.

When it comes to the recording, which takes place at AIR Studios in London, the track proves to be difficult. A first attempt on 3 October is put aside, the track is remade on 9 October and this time the result is the right one.

"Jet" is a catchy pop-rock song, built around the intro riff; it is galloping and effectively arranged, with a beefy horn section, a wall of electric guitars and a strong drum performance by McCartney, here at the top of his skills with a part filled with rolls and taken at a robust pace: it's the real rhythmic support to the track. On the two bridge sections, Paul beats on toms for an almost tribal-flavoured result.

The Minimoog D model (1970).

The Moog is employed in an ingenious way: the instrument plays just one long sustained note, which reinforces the bass with its buzz: this is a very economical part as well in terms of notes, both here and in the chorus, thus allowing the track to breathe. Only during the middle eight does the instrument plays its continuous line.

The essential solo at 2:03, which mirrors the verse melody with only slight variations is also the prerogative of the Moog. The vocal harmonies are captivating, with their almost burlesque tone and supported by some rhythmic footsteps, something that can be caught by listening to the separated tracks extracted from the videogame Rock Band. McCartney garnishes the whole song with a perfect vocal performance, full of enthusiasm: covered by the instrumental layers, there are handclaps, screams and sighs, proof of the passion with which Paul tackles the track in the studio. Also in this case, to fully appreciate these contributions the vocal part should be separated from the rest.

Since Paul wants a fleshier production, an orchestra and a powerful brass section complete the arrangement. But from a technical point of view, the final solo is the result of studio trickery. "At the end of 'Jet', there's a saxophone phrase that because of the awkward key, the key of A, couldn't be played on the tenor sax," Visconti says. "Luckily, the baritone player brought his alto sax, and he could play those top notes, but he couldn't play the bottom ones. So, at the end you hear a great deception. You actually hear two sax players, I don't know at which point the alto saxophonist stopped playing and Howie Casey began, but that's how it happened."[17]

Lyrically, the song is a showcase of daringly juxtaposed images, in the typical fashion of McCartney's lexical fantasy, with the odd reference to a suffragette possibly hinting at David Bowie's "Suffragette City". According to an article published by *Melody Maker* in the spring of 1973, "Suffragette" was the title of a song recently composed by McCartney, maybe "Jet". "I make up so much stuff," Paul says. "It means something to me when I do it, and it means something to the record buyer, but if I'm asked to analyse it, I can't really explain what it is. 'Suffragette' was crazy enough to work. It sounded silly, so I liked it."[18]

In an interview in 2017, Paul gave further details about the lyrics. Paul: "I wrote the song not about the puppy, but just using the name. And now it's transformed into a sort of girl. It was kind of – a little bit about the experiences I'd had in marrying Linda. Her dad was a little old fashioned and I thought I was a little bit intimidated, as a lot of young guys can be meeting the father figure. And if the dad's really easy-going, it makes it easy. It wasn't bad but I was a bit intimidated, probably my fault as much as his. Anyway, the song starts to be about the sergeant major and it was basically my experience, roughly translated. I never do a song with the actual words that actually happen, because then that's like a news story. 'Oh Linda, I was going to see your dad and he was intimidating.' A bit boring. So, I mask it and mould it into a song, something you can sing reasonably."[19]

From the "ride in the sky" of "Jet", which recalls the supersonic speed of aeroplanes, we now reach to the slow and irregular flight of "Bluebird", another episode in this anthology of freedoms represented by *Band on the Run*.

Musicians:

Paul McCartney vocals, backing vocals, bass, drums, electric guitar, piano • **Linda McCartney** backing vocals, Minimoog • **Denny Laine** backing vocals, electric guitar • **Howie Casey, Phil Kenzie, Dave Coxhill, Jeff Daly** saxophone • **Beaux Arts Orchestra** strings

* * *

Bluebird

(Paul and Linda McCartney)

Recording: 3 October 1973 (basic track), 8 October 1973 (overdubs part I) and 17 October 1973 (overdubs part II) **Location:** AIR Studios, London

McCartney's fascination for birds is something that goes back to his childhood. In Liverpool, young Paul develops a passion for ornithology and bird-watching thanks to an old handbook, *The Observer's Book of Birds*, by Stephana Vere Benson, whose first edition is dated 1937. "One of my hobbies is ornithology. In fact, I'm a keen ornithologist and always have been. As I've mentioned before, one of my favourite pastimes as a child was to take my *Observer's Book of Birds*, sit in the fields and lose myself in nature. I like me birds, as they say."[20]

"Bluebird" follows the tradition of McCartney songs dedicated to birds and it's the third in a rather extended sequence: preceded by "Blackbird" from the "White Album" and "Single Pigeon" on *Red Rose Speedway*, and to be followed later by "You Tell Me" (2007, *Memory Almost Full*, where a red cardinal is mentioned), "Two Magpies" (2008, *Electric Arguments*) and the quasi-instrumental "Long Tailed Winter Bird" (2020, *McCartney III*).

Perhaps it's not coincidental that the most exotic piece on *Band in the Run* has its origins in a place where nature is powerful and somewhere that would become one of McCartney's

The cover of *The Observer's Book of Birds*.

favourite tourist destinations. "I wrote it in Jamaica when we were on holiday," Paul explains, so "Bluebird" could indeed originate from December 1971 when Paul went with Linda on vacation to Montego Bay for the first time.[21] In fact, in the reproduction of McCartney's notepad included in the *Red Rose Speedway* Deluxe Edition, the title of the song is shown on the very same page as "Seaside Woman", written by Linda shortly after that sojourn. A detail that suggests a proximity in time for the composition of both songs.

If the song takes its cue from a real ornithological species, then "Bluebird" is not to be intended as the true name of the bird (which isn't present in the Central American country) but only as the generic description of a blue-coloured bird: in that case, it could be the Orangequat, endemic to Jamaica.

Recorded in its entirety at London's AIR Studios[22] (the basic track being laid down on 3 October 1973), "Bluebird" is an acoustic ballad in bossa nova style featuring a simple arrangement with a lovely tropical touch: the basic track consists of two acoustic guitars, bass, and many tinkling percussion effects, including güiro, sticks, cowbell, maracas, vibraslap, chimes and congas and probably also a rhythm box. The accent is on this rhythmic accompaniment, and in addition to that colourful percussive set, a very simple drum part is also featured.

The harmony is sweet, and McCartney tunes his guitar one step lower, to obtain more comfortable chord shapes: "'Bluebird' uses both major and minor chords, but also ones that have a little more complexity to them from adding another note on top of the regular chord," Paul says. "In 'Bluebird' I'm adding in a couple of sixths, which we learned about in The Beatles' early days and used to end some of our songs like 'She Loves You'. I'm also using a major seventh. The great thing about chords like these is that they don't sound rooted, they're quite free and give space and air to a song. They help get across the idea of flight and the feeling of a quiet evening when the wind is still."[23]

The acoustic guitar shifts between strumming (in the verses and in the refrain) and an arpeggiated part, employed in the chorus. The bass is sober, almost all played on cavernous tones: in some spots, it can be appreciated with embellishments as octave leaps (at 1:20), glissandos and scales (at 1:30).

The arrangement is enriched by some three-part harmonies by Paul, Linda and Denny Laine, very effective and well-orchestrated; in some sections they're sung in unison (in the verses, in the refrain and in the instrumental part), in others employing the contrapuntal technique of canon, where the voices chase one another, as in the chorus (where the three parts overlap and cross each other very smoothly) and in the ending, with a remarkable high note from Denny. The section underlying the sax solo is certainly the most evocative and boasts a different melody not heard anywhere else in the song.

McCartney's lead vocal is rich in nuance and relies on the technique called *portamento*: a sort of glissando used to gradually link two notes. In particular, it can be heard applied to the beginning and to the end of some words, to express additional sweetness and fluency.[24]

The percussion overdub takes place on 8 October. In a twist of fate, they're played by Remi Kabaka, a musician coming from Nigeria, although born in Ghana. "We went in Lagos intending to use some of the local musicians," McCartney confesses. "We started off thinking of doing a track with an African feel, or maybe a few tracks, using local congas players and African fellows. But when we're looking round and watching the local bands, Fela Kuti came up and said, 'You're trying to steal black music.' In the end we thought, 'We'll do it all ourselves.' The only guy from Africa is Remi Kabaka, someone we met in London. We discovered that he came from Lagos, but that was purely coincidental."[25]

For the percussionist it's a get-together. "Paul had been my friend for a long time," Kabaka says. "I was tight with Linda. She was my sister. You don't see people like her anymore. I don't even call her a woman; I call her a King Maker. Me and Denny went way back, before the Air Force. We had a band called Balls. Linda called me and told me to come to the studio. That cowbell you hear in 'Bluebird', that's me."[26]

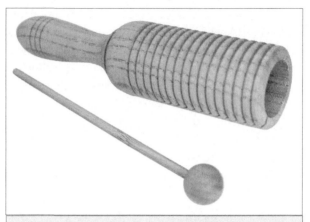

The güiro is an adaptation of an African or Latin-American musical instrument. It is played by rubbing a stick or tines along the notches to produce a ratchet sound.

That's not his only contribution: as was mentioned, in fact, many other percussion instruments can be heard. "If I remember correctly, we added things like a güiro, agogo bells, wood block, wind chime and shaker," [27] McCartney says. Kabaka could have contributed further to the percussion's rich section, possibly playing drums, since in a photo included on the Deluxe Edition of *Band on the Run* he is seen seated at the kit holding drumsticks.

The sax solo is by Howie Casey and is taped during the overdubbing session on 17 October. Things go down in an unusual way for the musician. "Paul said, 'I've got this nice ballad and I'd like you do play a solo on it'." Casey recalls. "He played the track, and I blew a solo, just coasting through it, looking at the chords. When we came to the end he said, 'That's it. That's fine!' I said, 'Hang on, Paul, I can do better than that'. He said, 'Maybe you can but that what I'm after.' He did let me try a few more times, but he used the first one and hearing it now, I can see he was right."[28]

It's a gem: Casey perfects his part not only through a variation on the main vocal melody, but overall playing it almost all in counterpoint. A poetic effect that enriches "Bluebird" with further magic: the solo seems to pop out from a moonlit night.

Lyrically, "Bluebird" is dedicated to the idea of flight as symbolic of escaping from everyday anguish, something beloved by McCartney and dealt with in other episodes in *Band on the Run*: the lightness of its melodic and harmonic structure creates a suggestive correspondence between words and music. It's the most delicate episode on the whole album. "The idea of flying has winged its way into some of my songs through the years, from 'Blackbird' in the sixties to 'Off the Ground' in the nineties, right through to the short-animated film I made for 'When Winter Comes' in 2020," Paul says. "I think the desire to be able to fly is fairly universal. Sometimes you wish you could just fly away from certain situations. It's quite a dreamlike idea."[29]

A fantasy subject that is masterfully painted by McCartney. "Bluebird" grasps what's difficult to grasp, tells what can't be told, with a combination of imagination and reality: love is the link. "One thing I really like is fantasising, dreaming about the perfect romance," Paul admits. "Because, generally speaking, you have to dream about it! So, I do enjoy imagining that perfect love in song and 'Bluebird' definitely falls into that category. I'm working with the distinction between 'what love can do' and not just 'what it's for'. I'm hoping to advance the idea that 'you will know what love is for.' As to 'what love can do': it can do all these wonderful things. There are sparkles everywhere. It's like a beautiful, magical dream. I am playing with the pure fantasy of this girl I have turned into a bluebird, which has a fairy tale quality of metamorphosis to it. It's not quite Ovid, but bluebirds are thought to mate for life, so there is an element of love and transformation in there. So now, what do we do? Are we going to just sit here or – seeing as we're birds and this is a fairy tale – why don't we fly away on an adventure together through the midnight air? We'll head across the sea."[30]

From one utopian space to the next, *Band on the Run* goes further in its search for an alternative world by offering purity free of social rules: "Leave me alone, Mrs. Vandebilt!"

Musicians:

Paul McCartney vocals, backing vocals, acoustic guitar, bass, drums (?), percussion (?) • **Linda McCartney** backing vocals, percussion (?) • **Denny Laine** backing vocals, acoustic guitar, percussion (?) • **Remi Kabaka** cowbell, güiro (?), conga (?), drums (?), agogo bells (?), wood block (?), wind chime (?), shaker (?) • **Howie Casey** saxophone

* * *

Mrs. Vandebilt

(Paul and Linda McCartney)

Recording: 10–14 September 1973 (basic track and overdubs part I), 17 October 1973 (overdubs part II) and 18–19 October 1973 (overdubs part III) **Location:** EMI Studios, Apapa (basic track and overdubs part I) and AIR Studios, London (overdubs parts II–III)

Charlie Chester, 1954.

What makes us feel freer than being surrounded by nature? What's more liberating than bursting into laughter? Well, "Mrs. Vandebilt" combines both: it's a hymn to carefree living and a return to Utopia, where man can really find release, in McCartney's view, "Mrs. Vandebilt" is conceptually one of the key tracks on *Band on the Run*.

The song gathers different ideas from a number of sources, and it's packed with references that show McCartney's passion for comedy and humour. The opening line "Down in the jungle / Livin' in a tent/ You use money / You don't pay rent / You don't even know time / But you don't mind" is an adaptation of "Down in the jungle, livin' in a tent, better than a prefab, no rent", a catchphrase made famous by comedian and presenter Charlie Chester in his BBC radio show *Stand Easy* (1946).

Also, the question "What's the use of worrying?" that recurs at the end of the verses seems to have a connection with the world of comedians. In fact, it could be derived from "Pack Up Your Troubles in Your Old Kit-Bag and Smile, Smile, Smile" an old World War I marching song, written by George Henry Powell and published in 1915: the song became very popular with British troops and contains the words mentioned above. McCartney could have been familiar with the song through the 1932 film *Pack Up Your Troubles* with Laurel & Hardy, of whom he was a big fan.[31]

The semi-serious tone of the verses resembles the grotesque and rather eccentric style of certain Gilbert O'Sullivan songs, whose humour and success in the early Seventies McCartney had admired.

Instead, the name of the title character pays homage to Gloria Vanderbilt (with an "r"), the noted artist and heiress from one of the richest New York families in the nineteenth century. "I didn't know anything about her," McCartney says, "but I just knew she was like … a rich person!"[32] This character allows its author to express his point of view about life and his values. "Mrs. Vandebilt is a figure of authority and wealth and rules and money that the protagonist of the song doesn't want to know about," Paul explains. "He wants to be left alone. And that's me, very much who I am."[33]

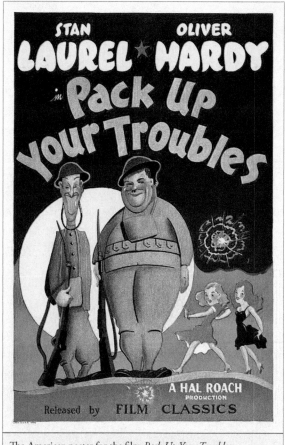

The American poster for the film *Pack Up Your Troubles*.

Gloria Vanderbilt, 1959.

The second chorus replaces "Mrs. Vandebilt" with "Mrs. Washington", very likely another allusion to the US, a place that Paul at the time could not visit due to his arrests for drug possession of the previous year and which prevented him obtaining a visa. Ironically, when *Band on the Run* is in the shops, McCartney's embargo has just ended. It's not difficult to believe that Paul changes the words to this chorus at the last minute, in view of that very coveted moment. A cry for freedom.

The track is taped in Apapa in September 1973, and in unfavourable conditions. "It was recorded during a power cut in Lagos," Paul reveals. "Suddenly everything went black and eventually we found ourselves doing it on EMI generated power and just hoping the hum wouldn't come over on the record."[34]

"Mrs. Vandebilt" is a rustic track, led by McCartney's powerful bass that seems to swing along with the agility of a gorilla on a creeper through the tangled jungle of Laine's acoustic guitar, the wooden sound of which seems deliberate. It's a walking bass kind of part, almost uninterrupted, that blends rhythm and internal hooks, and is very hummable. Among the other characteristic features of Paul's technique, we can highlight the glissandos, at 1:12, at 2:06 and at 3:22.

But the hook of "Mrs. Vandebilt" is without doubt the coarse "Ho Hey Ho", almost a derivation of the famous "Heigh-Ho" sung by the seven dwarfs in the Walt Disney animated film *Snow White and the Seven Dwarfs*. This expression, later changed to "Hey-Ho", has ancient origins and first appeared in print in 1471.

The song is rounded off by a dramatic refrain reinforced by Howie Casey's sax, whose melody was derived from "Mine for Me", a tune that McCartney would give to Rod Stewart in 1974. Casey plays the same riff an octave higher the second time around, although with a subtle imperfection in the latter, where the melody is very high pitched. The imperfection does not worry McCartney. "After 'Bluebird' Paul wanted me to play on 'Mrs. Vandebilt' so I did that," Casey says. "There was a bit of a squawk on one of the licks, but he kept it. He said, 'It sounds real …'"[35]

McCartney's drums are marked by a tight performance, with the distinctive feature of the tom cascades that accompany the acoustic guitar glissando. Another prime example of the blend of simplicity and effectiveness.

The song ends oddly with laughing and squealing – captured in Africa and then overdubbed in London in a session featuring Paul, Linda, Denny and various studio personnel – that completes the series of references to the comedy genre. It somehow seals the whole track.

"The laughing? It started off in Africa," McCartney recalls. "We were doing sort of daft laughs at the end. When we got back, we eventually overdubbed this crowd of people who were laughing. It was great listening to the tapes, trying to select the little bit of laughter that we would use. Most of it was us, but we need a little bit to cushion it up. It was great listening to a roomful of people laughing in stereo. They were getting into all these laughing bits, and we were on the floor!"[36]

A euphoric state which recalls the use of cannabis, of which Paul had admitted partaking. So, "Let Me Roll It" could be considered a paean to soft drugs, much like the earlier "Got to Get You into My Life".

Musicians:

Paul McCartney vocals, backing vocals, electric guitar, bass, drums, percussion (?) • **Linda McCartney** backing vocals, electric piano, percussion (?) • **Denny Laine** backing vocals, acoustic and electric guitar, percussion (?) • **Howie Casey** saxophone

* * *

Let Me Roll It

(Paul and Linda McCartney)

Recording: 10–14 September 1973 (basic track) and 10 October 1973 (overdubs)
Location: EMI Studios, Apapa (basic track) and AIR Studios, London (overdubs)

"Let Me Roll It" is a perfect example of the inspiration for a song and its recording being linked. It's another song which originates during a moment of relaxation for Paul, while he was immersed in nature in Campbeltown: "I wrote that up in Scotland on a nice day," McCartney says. "I was just sitting outside, plunking on a guitar and I got this idea for a song."[37]

No doubt the laid-back feel to the song is linked to its origins: "Let Me Roll It" has whiff of the blues, but McCartney style. Also, thanks to its simplicity, the track is committed to tape in Lagos without complication during the second week of recordings, although the features that will make it unique are recorded later in London.

"Let Me Roll It" is, in fact, essential rock/blues, centred on a powerful guitar riff that continues throughout the whole song. "We put down a backing track with Linda playing organ, me playing drums and Denny playing guitar," McCartney reveals. "Then we overdubbed the big guitars you can hear right the way through it, going through a vocal PA system to get the unusual guitar sound … not through a guitar amp but a vocal amp, it was a big powerful amp."[38]

Paul later tries to describe this instrumental part more clearly. "The single most significant element in this song … [is] the guitar riff," he says. "The word that comes to mind is 'searing'. It's a searing little thing. We can talk about lyrics till the cows come home, but a good riff is a rare beauty."[39]

The riff was overdubbed by McCartney at AIR Studios during the session of 10 October 1973. A very simple but carefully played part, whose almost heavy metal tone would prove fundamental over the decades when the track is played on stage, thus making "Let Me Roll It" a staple of McCartney's shows. "The lead guitar part is phenomenal, and it's even more amazing considering that it was double tracked," Emerick recalls. "Paul played that, and he did an excellent job of doubling the part with exactly the same phrasing and attitude. The guitar sound is a little reminiscent of John's ultra-distorted guitar in 'Revolution'. More eerily, there's a bad edit after the last chorus that adds an extra beat [at 4:22], just has happened on 'Revolution'…"[40]

Some time later, strangely enough, Paul would appear a little embarrassed. Answering a specific question by a journalist, he would reduce it to a not too successful attempt at sounding heavy: "In fact, if the truth be known, in my little subconscious, I got way too into all this 'trying to prove I can rock' over the last couple of years …,"[41] he admits.

Bass and drums are also typical of Paul's style. The bass is muscular, very high in the mix, and its simple line is key for supporting the track. The drums are very subtle: it's an elementary part, in 4/4, with hi hat, bass drum and snare. Drum rolls are only roughly sketched and, around 3:17, McCartney seems to miss a couple of bass drumbeats.

Many critics note some similarities between the track and Lennon's productions, such as the use of the tape echo on the vocals (Lennon's trademark, featured in songs such as "Instant Karma!" and "Mind Games") or the bare bones arrangement, reminiscent of the John Lennon/Plastic Ono Band album. Everything, including the oriental style guitar riff and a nasal vocalisation near the end (at 4:24), seems an affectionate homage to John. At first, Paul seems to deny the connection:" It was not really a Lennon pastiche, although my use of tape echo did sound more like John than me," McCartney says. "But tape echo was not John's exclusive territory …"[42] Later on, instead, Paul would refer to the echo as an intentional reference, labelling it the "bog echo", since it is similar to the echo in a bathroom (colloquially known as the "bog").

Whether this echo is intentional or not, "Let Me Roll It" soon starts a sort of virtuous circle of cross references and quotes with John. If its riff recalls "Cold Turkey", Lennon soon returns the compliment (or maybe tries to reclaim his riff?) and makes a copy of it in his instrumental track "Beef Jerky", which he releases the following year on *Walls and Bridges*.

Regarding the lyrics, Paul always denies any connection to Lennon, and confesses that the song was inspired by sharing a joint in good company, although not until 2010. "To tell you the truth, that was more [about] rolling a joint," McCartney says. "That was the double meaning there: 'Let me roll it to you.' That was more at the back of my mind than anything else."[43]

Musicians:

Paul McCartney vocals, backing vocals, bass, drums, electric guitar • **Linda McCartney** backing vocals, organ • **Denny Laine** backing vocals, electric guitar

* * *

Mamunia

(Paul and Linda McCartney)

Recording: 3 September 1973 (basic track) and 18–19 October 1973 (overdubs)
Location: EMI Studios, Apapa (basic track) and AIR Studios, London (overdubs)

And so on to side two. "Mamunia" opens it, almost a propitiatory chant to Paradise. Everyone back to Africa for a moment, then.

If McCartney's records are a kaleidoscope of influences, references and musical cross-pollination, one of their characteristics is that this aspect is never overwhelming. On the contrary, it stays in the background, it's a colour that's part of a wider palette, that is watered down and sacrificed on the altar of pop. It's included in Paul's giant songbook of popular music, where the various languages absorbed by him contribute each time to create the nuances needed for this or that track.

Band on the Run isn't an "ethnic" record, as Paul readily proved to Fela Kuti. For McCartney, Africa provides a certain mood, but does not necessarily have an impact on the arrangement of his music. "[Paul] thought it would be camp to go down there and maybe get an African influence," Vincent Romeo, McCartney's manager at the time, relates, "like when Dustin Hoffman was going to play a prisoner for *Papillon* and he went to prison to soak up the influence."[44]

The only exception is, to some extent, "Mamunia", the only Afrobeat-tinged track on *Band on the Run*. And the inspiration for the song, or at least its title, is African.

"Mamunia" is in fact inspired by a name that McCartney saw on two different occasions. "First it was the name of a hotel in Marrakesh where the whole band went for a holiday [in February 1973]," McCartney explains. "But it was spelt slightly different in that case [it's the famous luxury resort La Mamounia, that in Arabic means 'safe haven']. Then we saw it on a plaque on a wall in Lagos."[45]

Maybe it's not coincidental that this track launches the *Band on the Run* sessions in Nigeria, on 3 September. The recording takes place in quite unusual circumstances: "This was the first one we did in Lagos, recorded in the middle of a tropical rainstorm," McCartney recalls. "I don't know if that had any effect on the final result …"[46]

The lyrics sing the praises to the vital force of water, and specifically the rain element dominates the whole song, with the most varied references: from

Los Angeles clouds to a humid homely atmosphere. The term "plastic macs" (a reference to British mackintosh raincoats) refers back to "Penny Lane", where Paul uses the same word, which is also present in "The Ballad of John and Yoko".

Initially entitled "Ma Moonia", the song is based on acoustic guitars that play a radiant chord sequence, counterpointed by Paul's thumping bass. Without a real drum part, the rhythm is entrusted to some bass drum beats in the verse (according to some sources, supplied care of roadie Ian Horne) and to Laine's congas in the chorus. These are reinforced by shakers during the final section.

Harmonically, "Mamunia" is a three-part song, each being in a different key. The verse is in C, the chorus in in A, while the middle eight that opens at 3:00 modulates to G. Another noteworthy element is that the first two sections are both built on descending chord sequences.

McCartney's prominent bass part weaves throughout the song; kept very high in the mix, it's the cornerstone of the track. The playing is simple and charming, alternating sections in slight syncopation to others that underline the harmony. The three-part vocal harmonies are well-refined and are among the most characteristic of the whole album, with accompanying lines that both complete and integrate the main melody.

With its straightforward arrangement, "Mamunia" is cheerful: the singing of the band in the chorus evokes a festive ceremony in an African village. It peaks with the ending, Linda's glittering Minimoog solo and Paul's ebullient remark shouted off mike, between 4:19 and 4:22, that makes us understand he's having fun: "Everywhere I look it's the same old sound, I like it!"

Musicians:

Paul McCartney vocals, backing vocals, acoustic guitar, bass, shaker (?) • **Linda McCartney** backing vocals, Minimoog • **Denny Laine** backing vocals, acoustic and electric guitar, congas • **Ian Horne** bass drum

* * *

No Words

(Paul McCartney–Denny Laine)

Recording: 10–14 September 1973 (basic track and overdubs part I), 11–12 October 1973 (overdubs part II) e 17 October 1973 (overdubs part III) **Location:** EMI Studios, Apapa (basic track and overdubs part I) and AIR Studios, London (overdubs parts II–III)

The collage technique – by which Paul manages to combine different inspirations to form a song, thanks to his arranging skills – crops up everywhere in the album. "No Words" is another example: two ideas from Laine joined together and enriched by a middle eight from McCartney.

The song that caused the disagreement between McCartney and Henry McCullough during the August 1973 rehearsals, which resulted in the guitarist leaving Wings, finds a home on *Band on the Run*: it's the first songwriting credit by Laine in the group's history.

A typical case of collaboration, much like classic Lennon–McCartney. "I wrote the first few verses to 'No Words' and couldn't get any further," Denny says. "I took them to Paul, and he added his little bit of magic."[47]

The song dates back to the pre-*Red Rose Speedway* era. "It ended up being a dual composition, because 'No Words' was two songs that were put together," Laine adds. "It was Paul's idea to put two of my songs together, which made one song, and then he added a few lines in the last verse and helped me put it together. So, it came to be a dual composition. But basically, it was my song."[48]

This lyrical addition is worth investigating. McCartney's contribution to the lyrics has an obscure meaning, due to its intimate nature, but its sentimental value is inestimable. The words added by Paul in the last verse ("It's only me/I love you") refers to an episode that took place between him and John Lennon. "We were once having a right slagging session and I remember how he took off his granny glasses," McCartney recalls. "I can still see him. He put them down and said, 'It's only me, Paul.' Then he put them back on again, and we continued slagging … That phrase keeps coming back to me all the time. 'It's only me.' It's became a mantra in my mind."[49]

In another interview, Paul tells a similar story, completing it with the second half of the verse of "No Words", the expression "I love you", which he will use again in 1982 for "Here Today", the song with which he would pay homage to John, who has recently passed away. "Whatever bad things John said about me, he would also slip his glasses down to the end of his nose and tell me 'I love you'. That's really what I hold on to."[50]

Recorded at EMI Studios in Apapa between 10 and 14 September 1973, "No Words" is a melodic song with a Harrison feel to it, sung in tight harmony by Laine and McCartney, who adds a cherubic falsetto in the bridge that opens at 1:13. Here, his voice is only backed by a rhythm box and by some sparse bass drum hits, with a subtle accompaniment from electric piano and Moog.

On closer inspection, the bridge is nothing but a melodic variation on the harmony of the verse! In fact, it employs the same chord sequence (A–A7–G7–F#m–Bm–E–Fdim–A), but with an ascending tune in place of the more horizontal vocal line by Laine. A prime example of the polyphony art that McCartney masters, having few rivals in the pop music field.

The song is characterised by a certain richness of guitars, including the ascending riff – emphasised by a string quartet arranged by Tony Visconti and added at London's AIR Studios – and, near the end, some call-and-response solos that deserve to have been developed. Which in fact it was, since the complete version of the song is roughly two minutes longer: unfortunately, this still lies in the archives. Backing vocals are well crafted and feature the roadies Trevor Jones and Ian Horne in addition to the Paul–Linda–Denny trio.

The recording made in Apapa includes some details that are testament to, on the one hand, the need of a backing to help McCartney keep time, and, on the other, to a certain laxness in the recording quality. To help Paul, a rhythm box is featured on the track, as heard on other *Band on the Run* tracks, such as "Bluebird" and "Picasso's Last Words (Drink to Me)". Nevertheless, at some point McCartney misses a beat: the drum part is totally absent between 1:00 and 1:04, when he re-enters in extremis with a drum roll.

Laine puts his finger on it. "I think he got a lot of his style playing with Ringo, because Ringo's a very basic drummer," says Denny. "He doesn't overplay. He doesn't try to show off and put in too many fills. So, Paul just had that same approach to drumming. It's all about having a good feel and working with the vocal. I remember on 'No Words', Paul forgot one of his drum entrances and came in a measure too late. But we left it in and kind of built the arrangement around that."[51]

Perhaps trying to mask the performance's flaws, the drum's volume is kept low compared to other tracks on *Band on the Run*. Furthermore, some slight distortion seems to affect the guitar parts in many spots.

The next episode on the record seals the concept of freedom. "Picasso's Last Words" is emblematic to a certain expressive freedom of art. To "paint it" (it's appropriate to say), Paul involves one of the greatest contemporary artists, Pablo Picasso.

Musicians:

Paul McCartney vocals, backing vocals, electric guitar, bass, drums • **Linda McCartney** backing vocals, electric piano, Minimoog • **Denny Laine** vocals, backing vocals, electric guitar • **Ian Horne, Trevor Jones** backing vocals • **The Beaux Arts Orchestra** string quartet

❊   ❊   ❊

Picasso's Last Words (Drink to Me)

(Paul and Linda McCartney)

Recording: 17 September 1973 (basic track), 3–10 October 1973 (overdubs part I) and 17 October 1973 (overdubs part II) **Location:** Batakota Studios, Ikejia (basic track) and AIR Studios, London (overdubs)

A cubist pastiche, a puzzle that joins together musical snippets in the style of various Picasso periods, according to Paul, or "as flatulent an exercise as McCartney had ever concocted", in the opinion of critic Bob Woffinden? A song that manages to amaze an actor of the calibre of Dustin Hoffman or the most boring piece on *Band on the Run*? In any case, "Picasso's Last Words" remains a

Poster for the film *Papillon*. Released in December 1973, it met with great success, and was nominated for an Academy Award.

perfect example, to some extent even an astonishing example, of Paul McCartney's songwriting, based on improvisation and inspired by day-to-day life.

"Picasso's Last Words (Drink to Me)" is a song with a very specific origin and had an extraordinary witness in Dustin Hoffman. April 1973, and the actor is in Jamaica with Steve McQueen for the filming of *Papillon*, which contains scenes shot on various locations on the island, including the cliff of Negril and Falmouth. Paul and Linda are vacationing nearby, in Montego Bay, where they arrived on 12 April.

"We went down to Hoffman's house one evening, he invited us. We got to know each other a little bit," McCartney recalls. "A few days later we were sitting around with him, and we were talking about songs. He was saying, 'Where do you get them from?' I said, 'You really kind of pull them out of the air, they just come. You don't think too much about it, if they come great, they come great, if they come lousy, they come lousy'."[52]

Intrigued by that, the actor asks Paul if he really is capable of creating something from nowhere, just taking inspiration from any subject. "So he pulled out a copy of the *New York Times*," Paul recalls, "and said, 'This is something that turned me on, the last words Picasso said' [the article, entitled 'Pablo Picasso's Last Days and Final Journey', and was actually published in *Time* magazine, dated 23 April, reporting news of his death on 8 April 1973]. He read them out to me, 'Drink to me, drink to my health, you know I can't drink anymore'. It turns out he couldn't drink; he's an old bloke and the doctor advised him not to drink."[53]

Pablo Picasso's Last Days and Final Journey

DEATH holds no fear for me," Picasso recently told a friend. "It has a kind of beauty. What I am afraid of is falling ill and not being able to work. That's lost time." Right up to the end, Picasso lost no time.

The day before he died had been a day like many others at Notre-Dame-de-Vie, his hilltop villa at Mougins on the French Riviera. Late in the afternoon the artist had taken a walk in the little park that surrounds his sprawling stone house overlooking the reddish foothills of the Maritime Alps. He liked now and then to gather flowers and vegetables in the garden, often taking them inside to draw. "That day I showed him the anemones and pansies, which he particularly liked," recalls Jacques Barra, Picasso's gardener.

Later that evening Picasso and his wife Jacqueline entertained friends for dinner. Picasso was in high spirits. "Drink to me; drink to my health," he urged, pouring wine into the glass of his Cannes lawyer and friend, Armand Antébi. "You know I can't drink any more." At 11:30 he rose from the table

and announced: "And now I must go back to work." In recent weeks, he had been working especially hard, preparing for a big show of his latest paintings at the Popes' Palace in Avignon in May. On this night, before he went to bed, he painted until 3 a.m.

On Sunday morning Picasso awoke at 11:30, his usual hour, but this time he could not rise from his bed. His wife Jacqueline rushed in and then called for help. At 11:40, before a doctor could get there, Pablo Picasso was dead. Dr. Georges Rance, who arrived shortly afterward, attributed his death to a heart attack brought on by pulmonary edema, fluid in the lungs.

At daybreak on Tuesday, as an unseasonable snowfall blanketed the south of France, a small cortege left Mougins and carried Picasso's body to his 14th century château at Vauvenargues in the bleak Provençal countryside. Accompanying the body were Picasso's widow; her daughter by her first marriage, Catherine Hutin; and Paulo, 52, Picasso's son by his first marriage to the Russian dancer Olga Koklova. After the

110-mile journey, the mahogany casket, without ceremony, was placed in the château chapel to await the building of a mausoleum.

But the shroud of estrangement from three of his grown children that had clouded Picasso's last years also marred his death. For reasons never entirely clear, Maya, Picasso's daughter by his longtime mistress Marie-Thérèse Walter, and Claude and Paloma, his children by Françoise Gilot, had been prevented from seeing their father in recent years. Last week the same sad situation prevailed. Indeed, this time police were on hand to turn away Marie-Thérèse and other old friends who came to pay their respects.

Later that day, Maya, Claude and Paloma drove to Vauvenargues and placed a large wreath of vivid flowers on the cemetery overlooking the château. "That was as close to our father as we could get," Maya said. "It's sad. The whole situation is very delicate." The next day, Paulo's son Pablo, 24, of nearby Golfe-Juan, was reported in serious condition after drinking a bottle of chlorie acid. According to his mother (who has long been separated

The *Time* article which Hoffman hands over to Paul for "Picasso's Last Words".

Paul has his guitar with him, and the song quickly takes shape. "I strummed a couple of chords I knew I couldn't go wrong on and started singing, 'Drink to me, drink to my health,'" McCartney continues, "and he leaps out of his chair and says to his wife, 'Annie! Annie! The most incredible thing! He's doing it! He's writing it! It's coming out!'"[54] Years later, Hoffman would say this was one of the most memorable events of his life, right after the birth of his children.

As soon as he starts strumming, Paul gets an idea for a folksy song: "So, I started, thinking vaguely Dylan-y in my mind, in G, 'Drink to me, Drink to my health'," McCartney specifies. "Just imagine Dustin Hoffman, just like in his film, leaping up and down … He was just so amazed that he kind of gave me inspiration for that."[55]

Paul acknowledges a great debt to Hoffman. "I think what was nice is that he'd obviously seen those words as melodic himself," McCartney says. "He's an actor, so he understands the rhythm of the words, and I think when he read the quote, he might have thought, 'This flows beautifully.' It was a pleasure to do it, just to show off a little bit. I am lucky that it's something that comes naturally to me."[56]

The most incredible thing is that a tape witnessing that evening with Hoffman exists. Good practice for all songwriters is to have a recorder at hand in case ideas come out of the blue. But on this occasion the tape recorder belongs to Hoffman, and it proves to be useful. In his recollections of the Jamaican vacation, McCartney talks about two meetings with the actor: the first seems to be more superficial, just to get to know each other, the second is more extended and in depth.

On this second occasion, "Picasso's Last Words" takes shape. This recording, found by the daughter of Hoffman's personal assistant in the archives of the actor, does not capture the very moment of the creation of the song but the moments that immediately followed it, when the "Drink to Me" chorus is already recognisable. The portion of the tape made available so far also includes other songs: "Getting Closer" (released in 1979 on the album *Back to the Egg*), "Baa Baa Black Sheep" (a traditional English nursery rhyme), "Hands of Love" (from the recent *Red Rose Speedway*) and "Peggy Sue", a Buddy Holly classic, of which McCartney was enamoured.

Hoffman's reference to Picasso also finds such a prompt response from McCartney because the artist is an old acquaintance of his, so to speak. We find two hints at the great Picasso by Paul, both preceding the Jamaican episode.

On 13 January 1969, when The Beatles have been filming *Get Back* for ten days, Paul has a conversation with Michael Lindsay-Hogg, and mentions the 1956 documentary *Le Mystère Picasso* by Henri-Georges Clouzot (which Paul could have seen in early 1967, when the film was screened at the Academy Two cinema, not far from Abbey Road) as an analogous to the process the band is tackling for their own project, including the planned live concert: "They didn't sort of fast-cut the paintings or anything," Paul explains. "They showed how he built up, and they stayed on it."[57]

Some months later, in August 1969, Paul is at the hospital waiting for Linda to give birth to their first daughter, Mary. There he notices a picture on the wall, a reproduction of Picassos' painting *The Old Guitarist*. "I looked at it all week and thought, 'What chord's he playing?'" McCartney said in 1999. "I noticed it had just two fingers and I tried to see what chord it [was] and if it sound[ed] any good! I tried it as an inspiration and tried to write a song that only used two fingers."[58]

"Picasso's Last Words (Drink to Me)" holds a special place within the recordings for *Band on the Run* made in Lagos: not only is the was the last track recorded during the Nigerian sojourn but it's also the only one committed to tape at Ginger Baker's ARC Studios in Ikeja, in a rather odd session, to which the drummer himself contributes in an unusual way. "We got Ginger and a couple of people from around the studio," McCartney says, "and we got little tin cans and filled them with gravel from outside the studio, and used them as shakers, so at the end you hear this noise [from 5:02 until the end of the track], and that's Ginger and a big mob of us doing this gravel noise!"[59]

For Denny, it's like being back at home. "Ginger being there was great for me, because I felt more at home because I had a friend in the same town," he says. "We did go over to Ginger's one day just as a courtesy. Ginger put some sounds [on the session], if you like. He … actually played a fire bucket full of gravel for a shaker sound."[60]

"Picasso's Last Words (Drink to Me)", with its deliberately rambling structure, opens as simple acoustic folk (with Laine on lead vocals in the first verse) and builds up with the addition of a patchwork of themes taken from various other songs on the album, including "Jet" and "Mrs. Vandebilt". "We started off doing it straight. Then we thought, Picasso was kind of far out in his pictures," Paul says. "He'd done all these different kinds of things, fragmented, cubism, and the whole bit. I thought it would be nice to get a track a bit like that, put it through different moods, cut it up, edit it, mess around with it – like he used to do with his pictures. We tried to get in the song, sort of a cubist thing. So, we just made it all up and then edited the tape. There were about four or five big edits in it, really."[61]

"Picasso's Last Words" is put together with the safe hands of Emerick, who works with several edits. In fact, the track can be broken down in this way: 1. The acoustic heart of the song, with verse, chorus ("Drink to Me") and bridge (0:00–1:33). 2. Instrumental interlude (1:34–1:56). 3. Slowed down section, with drum machine, which also features strings, electric piano and a bass solo. In addition to the chorus, the vocals also hint at "Jet" (1:57–3.38). 4. "Drunken" chorus (3:39–4:09). 5. Shortened instrumental interlude (4:10–4:32). 6. Another slowed down section, again with the presence of the drum machine, this time in a shortened version (4:33–5:01). 7. Coda with the choral "Ho Hey Ho", taken from "Mrs. Vandebilt".

Again, it's worth highlighting McCartney's skills in building his drum parts with frugality over the course of the song, to compensate his relative deficiencies. Attentive listening reveals that there's no proper accompaniment in the first half: only some bass drum hits, and two inserts with hi-hat and snare, both short and with syncopation.

From 1:57 and until 3:38 (the first identifiable edit), on the other hand, the accompaniment is entrusted to a rhythm box, as in "No Words", while the drums use only the bass drum. At 3:39 the drums are featured, this time with some hits on toms, and at 4:33 the Korg is heard again, before shakers enter at 5:02. A distinctive trait is that cymbals are played backwards (0:21 and 0:46), as heard in the "swallowed up" sound.

Between 3:14 and 3:33 McCartney effectively performs a bass solo, a rarity in his discography. The two instrumental interludes are punctuated by a French dialogue, taken from the BBC radio programme *Le Flash Touristique* and spoken by Pierre Denis Le Sève: apparently, he had difficulty getting paid for his contribution but finally got a check for around £5. Between 1:34 and 1:54 can be heard: "*Ce que je souhaite, c'est que grâce à la campagne publicitaire de nombreux français en découvre les charmes. Je vous rappelle, notre service d'aide touristique est à votre entière disposition, vous savez nous envoyons gratuitement toute une série de guides, de listes d'adresses très utiles.*"

The chorus at 3:44 is sung as in a hostelry and is played at a slower tempo, with drunken quavering voices, background clamour, and shouts of joy.

Paul makes two requests of Tony Visconti to enhance the track. The elaborate string arrangement leads the track toward a different stylistic dimension. "Paul said, 'Just do your thing, but in the style of Motown strings,'"[62] the producer says, admitting later he was inspired instead by the style of composer Jack Nitzsche. This dreamlike addition can be heard in the two slowed down sections.

The second contribution that Paul requests, necessary for the instrumental interludes, requires a certain effort, due to McCartney's insistence. For this accompaniment, the arranger brings a clarinet and bassoon into play. "Paul came up with this wacky little pastiche of French music that might have been played on the radio around Picasso's time," Visconti remembers. "But he was obsessed with getting the bassoon part right and he kept asking the bassoonist to play more plummy!"[63]

With its kitsch atmosphere, "Picasso's Last Words" is a diversion from the classic McCartney song form. A pause before the fireworks, and a great ending.

Musicians:

Paul McCartney vocals, backing vocals, acoustic and electric guitar, bass, drums, electric piano, gravel cans • **Linda McCartney** backing vocals, gravel cans • **Denny Laine** vocals, backing vocals, acoustic and electric guitar, gravel cans • **Ginger Baker** gravel cans • **Unknown** gravel cans • **The Beaux Arts Orchestra** strings, bassoon, clarinet

* * *

Nineteen Hundred and Eighty-Five
(Paul and Linda McCartney)

Recording: 5 October 1973 (basic track), 17 October 1973 (overdubs part I) and 29 October 1973 (overdubs part II) **Location:** AIR Studios, London (basic track and overdubs part I) and Abbey Road Studios, London (overdubs part II)

A majestic finale is often a favourite of The Beatles and McCartney in particular, and so can't be missed on an album such as *Band on the Run*. "Nineteen Hundred and Eighty-Five" delivers a knockout punch.

A dramatic track, "Nineteen Hundred and Eighty-Five" derives its title from McCartney's need (and that of many pop composers) to find a good starting point to write a song, often just a rhyme; therefore, there is no connection with George Orwell's *1984*, as some critics have assumed. "With a lot of songs I do, it's all in the first line, and then you have to go on and write the second line," Paul says. "With this one it was 'No one ever left alive in nineteen hundred and eighty-five.' That's all I had of that song for months. ''No one ever left alive in nineteen hundred and eighty … six?' It wouldn't have worked!"[64]

The truth is that Paul is unable to finish the lyric and the song lies incomplete until the last moment, with the working title of "Piano Thing". The urgency of a recording sessions is necessary to force him to work on it: "This was originally a little thing I couldn't get words to, except for the first phrase," Paul admits. "But the words just came to me the day we were due to record, and I think it's turned out quite well!"[65]

This is the penultimate song recorded during the sessions at AIR Studios in London, on 5 October 1973: for the basic track and the following overdubs Paul plays piano, drums, and organ, Linda is on synthesizer and Denny on electric

Rolling Stones' single "We Love You", released on 18 August 1967.

guitar. The final vocal part is added at the eleventh hour, during the last mixing session, on 29 October 1973.

"Nineteen Hundred and Eighty-Five" is pulsating and urgent, built around a whirling piano riff very similar, for that matter, to the introduction to the Rolling Stones' "We Love You" (1967), which incidentally features Paul and John singing on backing vocals.

In truth, what Paul declares to be his inspiration is "Trouble Man" (1972) by Marvin Gaye, the main theme to the film of the same name. The relation between the two songs is distant, of course. As in the case of "Here, There and Everywhere", inspired by the Beach Boys, or "The Long and Winding Road", which Paul had written with Ray Charles in a corner of his mind. "If you hear the track we did and then you hear Marvin Gaye's track you probably would never know they were related," McCartney says. "I may be influenced by something, but it's in my head and doesn't necessarily show in the song."[66] In fact, a comparison between the two tracks reveals only a vague resemblance in the harmony and in some piano phrases, and the songs have a completely different pace, laid back in the case of Gaye, impatient in the case of McCartney.

The verses alternate with two breaks for organ and backing vocals, followed by an interlude where McCartney shows off his blues-tinged piano technique. His voice is impassioned, in line with the story narrated in the lyrics, fantastic and a bit obscure.

The smooth bass part takes some time to create, and McCartney opts for that style, even though he knows it has some flaws. "I did one engineering overdub when Geoff was out cutting 'Helen Wheels'," Swettenham recalls. "I think it was for the bass on 'Nineteen Hundred and Eighty-Five'. Paul kept on doing one little bit and he asked me, 'Is it any good?' and in the end he just said, 'Ah, that's fine' although it wasn't perfect."[67]

Again, McCartney manages the drum part with skill. The emphasis is on the bass drum and toms, and the use of cymbals is very limited. It is an interesting feature, in line with non-European cultures and sounds, to some extent pre-empting what Peter Gabriel would take to the extremes at the end of the decade, completely banning cymbals and rimshots from his album *Peter Gabriel III* thus leading the way to an ethnic concoction that would affirm him as one the most innovative and groundbreaking artist in the rock scene.

The track peaks in a striking finale, with an apocalyptic orchestral contribution. Visconti's arrangement, also added at AIR Studios, employs a pattern of rising notes over the harmony with its descending bass, and in its score, reproduced on the Deluxe Edition of *Band on the Run* in 2010 it reads: "Play a slight crescendo on every note".

The coda that opens at 3:43 is full of instruments, with overlapping phrases. In this section, between 4.30 and 4:50, a clarinet takes the lion's share of the arrangement, playing frantic phrases in jazz style. The recording of the clarinet happens almost by accident. "There's a clarinet solo at the end," Swettenham recalls. "They were doing the orchestral rehearsals, and the player started doing it by himself. And so, Paul asked him to do it again and they recorded it. I don't know if it was as good as the first time but that's what they kept."[68]

Laine lashes out a long electric guitar solo, while McCartney gives vent to some screaming vocalisations in the vein of "Hey Jude", for an enthusiastic ending. The track peaks in a striking finale, where strings, horns, synthesizer and guitar fuse together in a colossal euphony.

"Nineteen Hundred and Eighty-Five" ends with a *coup de théâtre*: a reprise of the chorus of "Band on the Run", that reinforces the idea of a common thread linking the album's songs. A suitable ending, in epic style, to an album and to an adventure that are both epic themselves.

Musicians:

Paul McCartney vocals, backing vocals, piano, bass, drums, electric guitar, organ, shaker (?) • **Linda McCartney** backing vocals, Minimoog • **Denny Laine** backing vocals, electric guitar • **Beaux Arts Orchestra** full orchestra

* * *

So, is *Band on the Run* proof that "art can triumph over adversity", as Mark Lewisohn noted? It's still a topic that's hotly debated, and Paul seems to be not fully convinced (although, of course, he offered a different view in more recent times): "When we got back, people would say, 'Ah, out of adversity has been born a good album,'" McCartney says in an interview. "I hate that theory. It may be true, as well. I hate the idea that you've got to sweat and suffer to produce something good. It turned out successful, anyway."[69]

Notes

1   Caroline Boucher, *Denny Laine Is The Lazy Star Who Doesn't Want A Hit Or A Glitter Suit*, *Disc and Music Echo*, 29 December 1973.

2   Caroline Boucher, *Denny Laine Is The Lazy Star Who Doesn't Want A Hit Or A Glitter Suit*, *Disc and Music Echo*, 29 December 1973.

3   Paul du Noyer, *Band on the Run* (Deluxe Edition) – *Paul McCartney Archive Collection*, 2010, p. 10.

4   Steve Marinucci, *Wings' 'Wild Life' & 'Red Rose Speedway': Denny Laine & Denny Seiwell Talk New Box Sets*, in *Billboard*, 26/12/2018, https://www.billboard.com/music/rock/denny-laine-denny-seiwellwings-box-sets-8491580/

5   Paul Gambaccini, *Paul McCartney in His Own Words*, 1976, p. 73.

6   https://www.youtube.com/watch?v=Cvh299W4h8k

7   *Band on the Run – 25th Anniversary Edition* (CD), 1999.

8   Paul McCartney, *The Lyrics*, 2021, p. 39.

9   *Goldmine*, 2001.

10   Mike Reed, *McCartney on McCartney*, BBC1, 1989.

11   Greg Schmidt, *The Victor Company | Geoff Emerick (EMI/HMV/Beatles) | His Master's Voice: Music Industry Interviews*, 18 January 2023, https://www.youtube.com/watch?v=C6czTmxnH_4

12   Paul Gambaccini, *Paul McCartney in His Own Words*, 1976, p. 80.

13   Keith Badman, *The Beatles. The Dream Is Over – Off the Record 2*, 2002, p. 120.

14   Wings Fun Club newsletter #4, August 1973.

15   Dermot O'Leary, *Paul McCartney and Wings: Band on Run*, ITV, October 2010.

16   https://www.youtube.com/watch?v=EIwW705Lr_s

17   Paul du Noyer, *Band on the Run* (Deluxe Edition) – *Paul McCartney Archive Collection*, 2010, p. 41.

18   Paul Gambaccini, *Paul McCartney in His Own Words*, 1976, p. 80.

19   Zan Rowe, *Paul McCartney Takes 5*, https://www.abc.net.au/triplej/programs/mornings/paulmccartney-takes-5-withhis-songbook/9228520, 06/12/2017.

20   Paul McCartney, *The Lyrics*, 2021, p. 677.

21   Keith Badman, *The Beatles. The Dream Is Over – Off the Record 2*, 2002, p. 120.

22   Author's interview with Pete Swettenham, 27 October 2014.

23   Paul McCartney, *The Lyrics* (Paperback edition), 2023, p. 39.

24 For a complete analysis of McCartney's lead singing and the vocal harmonies of "Bluebird" visit the YouTube channel "The Beatles Vocal Harmony" by Galeazzo Frudua: https://www.youtube.com/@TheBeatlesVocalHarmony

25 Keith Badman, *The Beatles. The Dream Is Over – Off the Record 2*, 2002, p. III.

26 Steve Roeser, *Talking Drummer: an Interview with Remi Kabaka*, July 2015.

27 Paul McCartney, *The Lyrics* (Paperback edition), 2023, p. 39.

28 Spencer Leigh, *Paul McCartney and Wings*, in *Record Collector*, no. 162, February 1993, p. 18.

29 Paul McCartney, *The Lyrics* (Paperback edition), 2023, p. 39–40.

30 Paul McCartney, *The Lyrics* (Paperback edition), 2023, p. 40.

31 An excerpt of the song can be heard during the TV show *James Paul McCartney* in a sequence shot in a Liverpool pub, where Paul is with his father and other friends and relatives.

32 Mark Lewisohn, *Wingspan. Paul McCartney's Band on the Run*, 2002, p. 70.

33 Paul McCartney, *The Lyrics*. 2021, p. 485.

34 Keith Badman, *The Beatles. The Dream Is Over – Off the Record 2*, 2002, p. 120.

35 https://thestrangebrew.co.uk/howie-casey/#comments

36 Paul Gambaccini, *Paul McCartney in His Own Words*, 1976, p. 80.

37 Keith Badman, *The Beatles. The Dream Is Over – Off the Record 2*, 2002, p. 121.

38 Keith Badman, *The Beatles. The Dream Is Over – Off the Record 2*, 2002, p. 121.

39 Paul McCartney, *The Lyrics*, 2021, p. 421.

40 Geoff Emerick, *Here, There and Everywhere. My Life Recording the Music of The Beatles*, 2006, p. 352.

41 Geoff Brown, *McCartney: There's Life after Death, Melody Maker*, 30 November 1974, p. 8.

42 Mark Lewisohn, *Club Sandwich*, no. 72, Winter 1994, p. II.

43 Simon Harper, *The Making of Paul McCartney. The Story of Band on the Run, Clash*, http://www.clashmusic.com/feature/the-making-of-paul-mccartney, 12 October 2010.

44 Adam Block, *McCartney: Beatle on Wings*, 1976. As reported in Allan Kozinn–Adrian Sinclair, *The McCartney Legacy. Volume 1: 1969–73*, 2022, p. 598.

45 Keith Badman, *The Beatles. The Dream Is Over – Off the Record 2*, 2002, p. 121.

46 Keith Badman, *The Beatles. The Dream Is Over – Off the Record 2*, 2002, p. 121.

47 Interview for Wings Fun Club newsletter, 2 May 1974.

48 https://www.songfacts.com/facts/paul-mccartney-wings/no-words

49 Hunter Davis, 3 May 1981, http://www.lastfm.it/group/Sir+James+Paul+McCartney/
    forum/217824/_/667947

50 Vicky Shaw, *John Lennon and I didn't fall out says Paul McCartney*, *The Independent*,
    https://www.independent.co.uk/news/people/news/john-lennonand-i-didn-t-fall-out-
    sayspaul-mccartney-1776918.html

51 Bill DeMain, *Denny Laine Interview*, *Guitar World*, January 2023.

52 https://www.youtube.com/watch?v=5vc9xcR61_I

53 https://www.youtube.com/watch?v=5vc9xcR61_I

54 Paul Gambaccini, *Paul McCartney in His Own Words*, 1976, p. 79.

55 Mike Reed, *McCartney on McCartney*, BBC1, 1989.

56 Paul McCartney, *The Lyrics*, 2021, p. 589.

57 https://theymaybeparted.com/2022/04/19/jan-13-picassos-last-words/

58 Michael Parkinson, *The Michael Parkinson Show*, 3 December 1999.

59 Paul Gambaccini, *Paul McCartney in His Own Words*, 1976, p. 79.

60 Kabir Bhatia, *From the Moody Blues to Wings to the Rock Hall: Q&A with Denny
    Laine*, 15 February 2023, https://www.ideastream.org/arts-culture/2023-02-15/
    from-the-moody-blues-to-wings-to-the-rock-hall-q-a-with-denny-laine

61 Paul Gambaccini, *Paul McCartney in His Own Words*, 1976, p. 79.

62 Tony Visconti, *Bowie, Bolan and The Brooklyn Boy*, 2007, p. 204.

63 Paul du Noyer, *Band on the Run* (Deluxe Edition) – *Paul McCartney Archive
    Collection*, 2010, p. 41.

64 Paul Gambaccini, *Paul McCartney in His Own Words*, 1976, p. 83.

65 Rosemary Horide, *Paul's Fun on the Run*, *Disc and Music Echo*, 8 December 1973,
    p. 20.

66 Paul Gambaccini, *Paul McCartney in His Own Words*, 1976, p. 66.

67 Author's interview with Pete Swettenham, 27 October 2014.

68 Author's interview with Pete Swettenham, 27 October 2014.

69 Paul du Noyer, *Conversations with McCartney*, 2015, p. 113.

— 7 —
"STAY STILL!": AN ICONIC COVER

P robably conscious of the need for something to match the quality of the recorded work, McCartney conceives a particularly memorable cover, which is realised at a special photo session that takes place on 28 October 1973 in Osterley Park, in west London.

The iconic photo is shot by Clive Arrowsmith, and depicts Wings together with six celebrities (John Conteh, Michael Parkinson, Kenny Lynch, James Coburn, Clement Freud and Christopher Lee) as escaping prisoners.

The concept for the cover is the result of an accident. "We were just lying in bed at night, as is our wont, thinking what shall we do for the album cover," Paul remembers. "We thought, *Band on the Run*, let's have a group of people caught in a spotlight as if they're trying to escape from jail. We thought, 'Well, we'll use actors', and then we thought, 'No, that's not going to mean much.'"[1]

Gathering a group of famous people is a spontaneous idea. "It was Linda … She said, instead of having some models, wouldn't it be great if each one of them was like a face you would recognise," Paul says. "So, we just literally got the phone numbers. I just liked James Coburn. I liked him from *The Magnificent Seven*."[2]

The group is contacted casually, as related by the actor mentioned by McCartney. "I was in town, and I guess it was Linda who called me," Coburn recalls. "She asked me if I was busy that day. As it was Sunday or something I said, 'No.' She told me what it was … And I thought, Paul McCartney? Why do they want me on the cover of this album? And I said, 'Sure, why not, I'd love to.' And so I did."[3]

After a good lunch at the Italian restaurant San Martino, owned by Silvano Setti, the nine gather in front of a wall near a building in Osterley Park for the photo. Which proves to be more complicated than expected. The photographer recalls how it went, and that, from a technical point of view, the final result features an error: "This was one of my first photographic jobs when I was still an Art Director," Clive Arrowsmith says. "I had known Paul McCartney and John Lennon from my art school days and Paul asked me to shoot the cover of his new Wings album *Band on the Run*. With only enthusiasm and not much experience I went for a meeting with Paul and his art director the late great Storm Thorgerson from Hipgnosis. Paul and Storm talked through the basic concept that surprisingly the 'band was on the run' and we all agreed that the best way put this across was like an old fashioned 'Hollywood prison break movie' with the convicts in a spotlight against the prison wall (with additional celebrities as convicts)."[4]

The organisational side is far from perfect, and a first issue is the lightning. "On the day I hired a spotlight from the lighting company which, unfortunately, was not powerful enough for the job," Arrowsmith reveals. "This meant that everyone had to be very still for over two seconds for the picture to be sharp. Two seconds may not sound like a long time; however, they did have a party before the shoot and everyone was very much the worse for wear, but still enjoying each other's company to say the least."[5]

Having the group hold a static pose is a hard task. "Trying to get everyone to stay still and play the part of escaping prisoners was proving extremely difficult, amid the laughter, jokes and substance haze," Arrowsmith recalls again. "I arranged them all together so they could lean against each other and the wall. Now, because they had all become a little unsteady on their feet, Denny Lane fell over a couple of times laughing hysterically – everyone was having a great time. I had to have a megaphone to get their attention, I had even positioned myself up to the top of a ladder, next to the spotlight and barked instructions persistently, which the most part everyone ignored, until I finally snapped and screamed 'Stay Still!'"[6]

It isn't over. "I only managed to shoot two rolls of film, which is only 24 exposures in total," Arrowsmith says. "The group couldn't hold the pose for long, some would be still in one frame and others would be moving in another, the real worry was that there wouldn't be a shot where everyone was still and sharp. My woes did not end there, once the film came back it had a strong warm yellow cast but thankfully there were four frames where everyone was sharp. I showed them to Paul, and he loved them, I never mentioned the golden hue to him until a few years later when I was photographing the back cover for *Wings at the Speed of Sound*. After the shoot, over coffee, I said, "Paul, there is something I've meant to tell you for years, that yellow light on the *Band on the Run* cover? That was a mistake. I used daylight film instead of tungsten," Paul laughed and said, "That's fine, I thought it looked great and that you meant to do it."[7]

It is a high-spirited day, despite the heavy rain. "Clive Arrowsmith, the photographer, ran out of film on the shoot, and that's why it ended up with that sepia colour," Denny Laine remembers. "He'd put in a different kind of film, and it was a fluke that he got that certain lighting. Sometimes life's like that, where

The cover of the album. From left to right: Michael Parkinson, Kenny Lynch, Paul McCartney, James Coburn, Clement Freud, Linda McCartney, Christopher Lee, Denny Laine and John Conteh.

you come up with something special by accident. It was a fun day. Very up and positive. For me, the big surprise was finding out that [actor] Christopher Lee was a huge music fan and knew about records and stuff. The only direction was, 'Okay, make believe you've been caught in the spotlights by the prison guards.' Everybody looked one way, and funnily enough, I looked the other way."[8]

The fame that derived from that appearance on the record cover will pursue its protagonists for decades. "The oddest thing happened to me was about [1995 or 1996]," Clement Freud recalls. "So, the record had been out for 22 years, during which time I had grown a beard, aged, put on weight … and I was in San Diego, and a man stopped me in the street and said, 'Hey, you are in the cover of *Band on the Run*.' And I walked on, and he ran up to me and said, 'Who are you?' And he had actually recognised me from a bit part on a record cover."[9]

Notes

1   Paul Gambaccini, *Paul McCartney in His Own Words*, 1976, p. 73.

2   *Band on the Run – 25th Anniversary Edition* (CD), 1999.

3   *Band on the Run – 25th Anniversary Edition* (CD), 1999.

4   https://clivearrowsmith.org/2014/01/13/
band-on-the-run-the-great-wrong-film-debacle/

5   https://clivearrowsmith.org/2014/01/13/
band-on-the-run-the-great-wrong-film-debacle/

6   https://clivearrowsmith.org/2014/01/13/
band-on-the-run-the-great-wrong-film-debacle/

7   https://clivearrowsmith.org/2014/01/13/
band-on-the-run-the-great-wrong-film-debacle/

8   https://www.guitarworld.com/features/denny-laine-paul-mccartney-and-wings

9   *Band on the Run – 25th Anniversary Edition* (CD), 1999.

— 8 —
PROMOTIONAL INITIATIVES

The efforts by McCartney and the record company to promote *Band on the Run* are a classic combination of different initiatives, which yielded astonishing results.

First of all, Paul himself takes the field in a big way, granting numerous interviews. From the end of October and until the end of 1973, a real barrage of interviews for British radio stations and specialised press begins. On 27 October,

The cover of *Rolling Stone*, 31 January 1974, with Paul and Linda.

Promotional page in *Disc and Music Echo*, 8 December 1973.

New Musical Express leads the dance; on 24 November McCartney guests on *Capital Radio* for the Kenny & Cash Show; on 1 December three press interviews for *Sounds*, *Record Mirror* and *Melody Maker* are published; on 7 December it is the BBC's turn, while on 8 December *Disc and Music Echo* provide a delightful end.

With the coming of 1974, McCartney opens up the throttle. This change of pace is represented in the American stage. On the one hand, Paul hints at the chance of again working with John, George and Ringo, a scenario made more plausible after Allen Klein had left the reins of Apple: we can find at least two statements by McCartney on this topic, the first in an article in the *New York Times* (January), the second in a TV interview aired by NBC in March.

On the other hand, Macca and his missus are on the cover of the 31 January 1974 issue of *Rolling Stone*, which contains what can be considered the most revealing and in-depth interview of his entire career, granted to Paul Gambaccini. The conversation not only reviews McCartney's career with The Beatles, as a solo artist and with Wings, but also explores many aspects of his personal life, from his musical education to his parents, from his relationship with John Lennon to the various aspects of his character. Extremely significant is that the cover features only Paul and Linda.

* * *

Numerous pages promoting *Band on the Run* appear in the press at the time of the release of the album. They feature two different artworks, depending on the market: the first was reproduced in both *Disc and Music Echo* (8 December 1973)

Billboard, 8 December 1973.

and *Record Mirror* (14 December 1973), and depicts the bar of a jail broken in the middle, where the cover of the album appears.

The second, aimed at the US market, appears in *Billboard* on 8 December 1973. It has just the cover of the album, on a black background, accompanied by "Paul McCartney – Wings", with the label (Apple) and the record catalogue number written on it.

* * *

Last but not least *Band on the Run* owes much, if not everything, to the release of two singles. The strategy for their launch deserves a detailed analysis by itself, and still today remains the most successful example of synergy between product and marketing within McCartney's career.

— 9 —
WE'LL GO FOR A RIDE IN THE SKY: THE COMMERCIAL SUCCESS

*B*and on the Run is released on 30 November 1973 in the UK and on 5 December in the US. Bolstered by two singles that were released with perfect timing, the album becomes a huge success, reaching the no. 1 spot both in the US and in the UK.

So, *Band on the Run*'s commercial success intertwines with the release of its singles, and it's a classic story. We can truly say it's a case study in discography marketing (and not only that). In fact, without a driving single the album initially struggles somewhat.

It takes decisions by Capitol's marketing department to change its fate: on the one hand, by including "Helen Wheels" in the US version of the album, on the other by launching two singles, "Jet" and "Band on the Run", that become million sellers and push *Band on the Run* to no. 1 in the charts during spring and summer of 1974, more than six months after its initial release.

* * *

The "prologue", so to speak, concerns "Helen Wheels" in the US. The track is not included on *Band on the Run*, but is released as a single instead, a few weeks before the release of the album. "I got a call from the company saying we were 'missing a natural marketing opportunity'," McCartney later recalls. "I said that the song wasn't written for the album. But finally, reluctantly I said, 'Ok, put it on the album but bury it on side two'."[1]

That "someone" from the record company is not just anyone. He's no less than Al Coury, at the time Vice President of Capitol and head of the marketing department in Los Angeles. Easily considered the best promoter of all times, *Time* labelled him "The Man Who Sells the Sizzle".

"In those days he had a visa problem [a minor marijuana bust in England] and couldn't come to America," says Coury. "He'd send us tapes through the mail, with the label copy and everything, and we'd put the thing out. He'd send us ads, and we would work it. Anyway, Paul put out 'Helen Wheels,' and it went to Number One [Coury's recollection is inaccurate]. The next thing, the label copy for the album *Band on the Run* came, and it didn't include this hit. I couldn't understand that."[2]

The promoter calls McCartney, who told him that "Helen Wheels" didn't fit into the album's concept. "But," says Coury, "he allowed me to put it on the LP, based on the fact I was very strong and demanding."[3]

Notwithstanding Coury's recollections, looking at the dates it's difficult to conclude that the decision is taken after the success of the song in the US; more likely is that it was due to the simple fact of the single not being included in the album.

In fact, "Helen Wheels" enters the charts at no. 66 on 24 November 1973. The top spot is, happily, "Photograph" by Ringo Starr, the single taken from his album *Ringo*. The following week, McCartney's track jumps 20 positions and reaches no. 42, while the Top Three is: "Top of the World" (Carpenters), "Photograph" (Ringo Starr), "Goodbye Yellow Brick Road" (Elton John).

On 8 December, when *Band on the Run* has just hit the stores, "Helen Wheels" is at no. 31; on 15 December it's at no. 24, on 22 December it's at no. 20, and on 27 December at no. 16. A regular progression that peaks at no. 10 in the week of 12 January 1974. The single remains in the chart until 16 February, with a run of thirteen weeks on the *Billboard* charts.

*　*　*

Later, it is Al Coury again who changes the fate of *Band on the Run*. For the second time, he pushes McCartney in terms of marketing, insisting on a new single, which he considers the commercial heart of an album. "Paul didn't want any singles from *Band on the Run*," Coury reveals. "Shortly after we released the album, we started to get some heavy response from pop radios on the track 'Jet', and they started to edit the song."[4]

McCartney agrees to the preparation of an edit, even though he does not take part himself. A diplomatic incident could have undermined the Capitol promoter's brilliant work, however. "Paul came to Los Angeles because his song from the James Bond movie ['Live and Let Die'] was nominated for an Academy Award," Coury says. "Meanwhile, I realised that he never heard the edit. We called up radio stations in L.A. and told 'em not to play that song while he was in town. He was driving down Sunset Boulevard, and he heard the edited version of 'Jet' on the radio. He hated it. He pulled over to the side of the road, got into a telephone booth and called up his manager, who called me up and was just crazy because Paul was crazy. So, I said, 'You tell Paul that the record he heard was an edit the radio station did.' Which apparently Paul accepted, and which could very well have been true. I really don't know what edit he heard. And I got off the hook."[5]

Promo poster for "Jet". The claim "Destination: # 1" would prove optimistic, but the single is a smash.

Coury is proved right. "Jet" reaches no. 7 both in the US (with sales for over one million copies) and in the UK (200,000 copies), pushing *Band on the Run* back up the charts: in the course of a few days, the album's sales in the US jump from 700,000 to 1,500,000 copies.

The single enters the *Billboard* chart at no. 69, on 9 February 1974: that week, the Top Three spots feature at no. 1 "Love's Theme" (Love Unlimited Orchestra), at no. 2 "The Way We Were" (Barbra Streisand) and at no. 3 "You're Sixteen" (Ringo Starr is back). The following week, while "Helen Wheels" is still in the charts (at no. 58), "Jet" leapfrogs it to no. 47. The push from radio is clearly strong, as on 23 February "Jet" gains other twenty spots. At the top, there's Streisand.

On 2 March, "Jet" reaches no. 20. The time is ripe for its entrance into the Top Ten. The following week the track is at no. 14, and on 16 March is at no.

Sticker for the single "Jet".

10. The sequence proceeds as follows: 8–7–11–14–27–38 (on 27 April, when the second single "Band on the Run" has already entered the charts and is only three spots below) –47–48. "Jet" is certified Gold by the R.I.A.A. for one million copies sold.

Meanwhile, in the UK "Jet" reaches no. 7, with nine weeks in the charts and a healthy 200,000 certified sales: in April, *Band on the Run* goes to no. 2 – its best position up to that moment – while the single is at the peak of its popularity.

The single cleans up in Japan (selling over 117,000 copies) and reaches the Top 10 in Canada, Germany and Norway. "Jet" is heavily promoted: a video is created for Dutch TV including pictures of Paul and Linda alternating with the song's lyrics, an advertisement is published in *Billboard* and a sticker is also prepared: it shows a girl with the word "Jet" across her naked breasts and the command "Expose it!"

* * *

The second single taken from the album is its title track, and again the results are sensational. "Band on the Run" is released on 8 April 1974 in the US: the single is a smash and goes to no. 1 on *Billboard*.

For this single as well, the role of the marketing department is fundamental. To guarantee the best radio airplay, an edit of the song is prepared, shortening it from 5:08 to 3:50. This is not an easy task, due to the three-headed nature of the track, but "Band on the Run" is too tasty a morsel for the singles market to ignore. "If you can put out a title track, then you have the greatest marketing tool you can imagine," Coury is to claim. "But the track had three separate movements and it ran over seven minutes [Coury is wrong, as the song is only 5:08 in length]: so, it became almost impossible to do. I convinced Paul to let me do an edit: 'I'll keep the three movements in there, but let me do an edit on the seven-and-a-half-minute track, OK?' Anyway, John Palladino [Capitol's engineer] did an edit on 'Band on the Run' that's so unbelievable that it blew Paul McCartney away. He couldn't believe that anybody could cut those three pieces and put them together and make them still represent the beginning, middle and end of what that song was all about."[6]

Let's follow the trend of the single on the US market. "Band on the Run" debuts on 20 April at no. 68, while the top spot is held by "TSOP (The Sound of Philadelphia)" by the soul group MFSB, pursued at no. 2 by Elton John's "Bennie and the Jets", which was at no. 1 the previous week.

Cover for the US single "Band on the Run".

On 27 April, Paul McCartney and Wings' single is already at no. 41, but among the top spots is another ex-Beatle: yet again it's Ringo, who is at no. 5 with "Oh My My". On 4 May 1974, "The Loco-Motion" by Grand Funk Railroad removes "TSOP (The Sound of Philadelphia)" from the top spot and "Band on the Run" moves up to no. 22 (with "Jet" still in the charts, at no. 47). On 11 May, nothing changes at the top, but McCartney's single is now at no. 14.

The progression continues: no. 7, no. 5, no. 2 (behind "The Streak" by Ray Stevens) and finally no. 1, on 8 June. From there, the single notches up other eight weeks in the Hot 100 (with the following sequence: 5–6–8–17–15–26–40–60–70–95). Total: 18 weeks in the charts and two million copies sold!

Even in the UK, where the single is released later, on 28 June (with an unreleased track on its B side, "Zoo Gang", an instrumental composed by McCartney as the main theme for the TV series with the same title), "Band on the Run" does very well, peaking at no. 3 (with eleven weeks in the Official Chart) and a good 250,000 units sold.

* * *

These are the reasons behind the unprecedented success of *Band on the Run*. The album remains in the US and UK charts almost continuously for more than two years.

Let's retrace this run, starting from the US charts, since it's a prime example of winning a synergy between marketing initiatives and product quality.

Band on the Run debuts in the charts during the busy Christmas period, on 22 December, at no. 33. The Top 5 is as follows: no. 1 *Goodbye Yellow Brick Road*

On Wings Of Gold

HOLLYWOOD — One week after its release, Band on the Run, the new album by Paul McCartney and Wings, has been certified gold by RIAA based on sales through Dec. 5. The million-dollar seller by group members Paul McCartney, Linda McCartney and Denny Laine is on the Apple label, distributed by Capitol Records. This is the fifth gold album for McCartney since the dissolution of the Beatles, the previous LPs being McCartney (Paul McCartney), Ram (Paul and Linda McCartney), Wild Life (Wings), and Red Rose Speedway (Paul McCartney and Wings).

The news of the RIAA Gold certification for *Band on the Run*.

The poster in *Record Mirror* on 27 July 1974 to celebrate *Band on the Run* reaching no. 1 in the UK.

(Elton John), no. 2 *The Joker* (Steve Miller Band), no. 3 *Ringo* (Ringo Starr), no. 4 *Jonathan Livingston Seagull/Soundtrack* (Neil Diamond), no. 5 *Quadrophenia* (The Who). The following week McCartney's album rises to no. 21, then goes to no. 14 and to no. 13, reaching no. 9 in the week of 19 January 1974. A further eight weeks in the lower part of the Top Ten follow (no. 8–7–9–8–9–9–8–8–7), with a jump to no. 5 on 30 March, when the single "Jet" reaches its peak, and another leap to no. 2 the following week. In the meantime, the top spot has been held by albums including Bob Dylan's *Planet Waves*, Barbra Streisand's *The Way We Were* and John Denver's *Greatest Hits*.

BPI certification for *Band on the Run* sales in the UK.

John Denver is overhauled on 13 April. The push given by the first single has achieved its results. But it's not over. The second single "Band on the Run" has been just released and the album keeps on running. After another seven weeks in the Top Ten (2–4–7–7–6–4–2), where the soundtrack to *The Sting* dominates, on 8 June *Band on the Run* is back at no. 1, removing Scott Joplin and Marvin Hamlisch's album and keeping the top position for a further week.

The record holds no. 2 for two weeks before going back to no. 1 on 6 July. The album manages to reach the no, 1 spot in three different occasions. From then until the end of the year, there are seven more weeks in the Top Ten (4–4–7–8–10–10–10). It's 31 August before the album leaves the Top Ten: seven and a half months have passed since its entrance in the Olympus of the bestselling records. In total, *Band on the Run* would spend 124 weeks on *Billboard*'s chart.

The album is also an outstanding success in the UK, with a run of 116 weeks in the charts. The record also reaches no. 1 in McCartney's homeland, where it remains for seven weeks. During 1974, only the Carpenters (*The Singles 1969–1973*) and Elton John (*Greatest Hits*), do better, both with 11 weeks at the top spot.

The story of *Band on the Run* in the UK charts is interesting to follow in its main stages as well. The album enters the charts (unlike the *Billboard 200* album chart, the UK album chart at this point is a Top 60) at no. 45 on 15 December 1973, when David Cassidy holds the top spot with *Dreams Are Nothing' More Than Wishes*. The week before Christmas, *Band on the Run* has already entered the Top Ten (at no. 9), a placement that is also confirmed in the following week. A small drop at the beginning of 1974 (no. 13 and no. 11) preludes a great resurgence: starting from 19 January, McCartney's album amasses 27 weeks in the Top Ten, peaking three times at no. 2. The first happens on 30 March, when it settles between the Carpenters' *The Singles 1969–1973* and Elton John's *Goodbye Yellow Brick Road*, the second on 4 May, with the same trio of albums, and the third on 20 July: this time the top spot is by *Caribou* (by the ubiquitous Elton John) while no. 3 is held by another Seventies classic, Mike Oldfield's *Tubular Bells*.

And suddenly we're there: on 27 July *Band on the Run* finally reaches the top spot. Over the seven consecutive weeks in which the album sticks to no. 1, it holds off a challenge from *Tubular Bells*. On 14 September, *Band on the Run* is finally unseated by Mike Oldfield: but, irony of fate, it is by his new record *Hergest Ridge*, which leaves *Tubular Bells* at no. 2!

Band on the Run stays in the Top Ten continuously until 16 November 1974. After that, it progressively slips, but remains in the charts until 29 November 1975. Over the course of 1976, the record experiences a second youth, and notches up another 19 weeks in the charts! The last one is on 13 November, almost three years after its release.

In America, the record would be certified triple Platinum by the RIAA, while in the UK *Band on the Run* sold around 750,000 copies.

The album is no. 1 also in Canada, Australia, Spain and Norway. It's no. 4 in Belgium, no. 5 in Netherlands and Sweden, no. 11 in Japan (125,000 copies sold). We have two certifications from other countries: 100,000 copies in France and 80,000 copies in New Zealand (no. 23 in the charts).

The following reissues confirm its enduring popularity: the 25th Anniversary Edition of the album, released in 1999, re-entered the charts at no. 69 in the UK, while the 2010 edition from the *Paul McCartney Archive Collection* sold 125,000 copies in the US (no. 29 on *Billboard*) and was certified Gold by the BPI for 100,000 sales in the UK, where it peaked at no. 17 and spent five weeks in the charts. The 50th Anniversary Edition reached no. 16 in the UK and no. 156 in the US.

Following the tradition of diversifying the singles for markets, the record company also releases "Mrs. Vandebilt" for continental Europe and Australia in January 1974. It's not as resounding a success as the other two singles, but nevertheless reaches no. 7 in the Netherlands and no. 19 in Belgium.

To date, *Band on the Run* is McCartney's best seller, although statistics are not precise. Paul McCartney's official website reports seven million copies sold, although many sources mention five million copies already at the end of the Seventies. In 2024, a report by Allan Jones for *Music Week* reveals that the official total sales of *Band on the Run* for the UK amount to 1,587,000 copies.

And to think that, initially, Paul was worried about sales. "When it started off, it moved very slowly," McCartney recalled. "It got up to about number seven in the American charts and then started to drop down. I thought, 'Oh God, here we go again, I'd better leap into the studio and think of something else'."[7]

Notes

1   Paul du Noyer, *Band on the Run* (Deluxe Edition) – *Paul McCartney Archive Collection*, 2010, p. 64.

2   Ben Fong-Torres, *How RSO's President Spread 'Saturday Night Fever'*, Rolling Stone, Issue 275, 5 October 1978.

3   Ben Fong-Torres, *How RSO's President Spread 'Saturday Night Fever'*, Rolling Stone, Issue 275, 5 October 1978.

4   *Band on the Run – 25th Anniversary Edition* (CD), 1999.

5   Ben Fong-Torres, *How RSO's President Spread 'Saturday Night Fever'*, Rolling Stone, Issue 275, 5 October 1978.

6   Paul du Noyer, *Band on the Run* (Deluxe Edition) – *Paul McCartney Archive Collection*, 2010, p. 64.

7   Rosemary Horide, *School, My Kids and Me, Disc and Music Echo*, 7 November 1974.

— 10 —
"PAUL McCARTNEY IS BACK!": CRITICAL RECEPTION AT THE TIME OF RELEASE

t's interesting to analyse the critical reception to *Band on the Run* at the time of its release. Does its acclaim predate, accompany or follow the success of the record? To what degree is one determined by the other?

Looking at the dates, we can affirm that the critics immediately sense that the album is a classic. The earliest review appears on *Billboard*, the music industry mouthpiece, which assigns its "Spotlight" to the record on 8 December 1973, on the page dedicated to the new releases and writes:

> "This LP … is artistically an impressive work. … Concern and care are the hallmarks of this outstanding package." The weekly magazine also reviews some of the tracks. "'Jet' is a song with strong overtones of The Beatles – more so than any previous McCartney effort with his band. … McCartney and Linda team on the simple, innocuous 'Bluebird' and their harmonic construction turns the tune into an infectious listening experience."

In the UK, on 19 January 1974, NME labels it "a master stroke" and heralds it as "one of the best LPs of the year".

The *New York Times* has no doubts about the record:

> "What are Jason Robards [sic], James Coburn, Clement Freud, Paul and Linda McCartney (who is a dead ringer for David Bowie) doing on the cover of Paul McCartney's brand-new album, *Band on the Run* (Apple SO-3415)? Apparently, they're escaping from prison if I read the title tune correctly, but I don't think it really matters. It's the sound in the grooves that grabs you.
>
> McCartney, his wife and guitarist Denny Laine (the only musician left from McCartney's Wings) have made an album bursting with a great deal of compelling music even if the lyrics at times make as much sense as that cover photo. Undoubtedly there are those who will get so caught up in trying to analyze lines that they won't hear the musical dynamics. That's a very

real danger, in printing the lyrics – particularly if you're an ex-Beatle and the world expects you to be meaningful with a capital M. McCartney's real meaning lies in the sound which is woven out of various vocal and instrumental colours."[1]

In March 1974 *Circus*, in an article by Janis Schacht, writes:

"It's been such a long time since anyone of the mighty foursome has given us something to really scream about. I mean, sure, by comparison with most of the stuff that comes out of John, Paul, George and Ringo have been excellent, but, compared to their united efforts of yesteryear, they've been nothing.

Now, Paul fans, you may scream, screech, and yes, rejoice. *Band on the Run* is absolutely brilliant. From the first strains of the title track there is an obvious difference. Suddenly all the subtleties of McCartney melody lines are back. And the vocals? Not since Abbey Road has Paul delivered such clear and satisfying performances. The album is credited to Wings, but for the first time this is a Paul McCartney album, and no one gets in his way or mars the full effect.

'Jet' roars in, leaving little time to notice the transition from 'Band on the Run.' All of a sudden, the room is filled with soaring harmonies, raunchy, rocking riffs and clever, distinctly McCartneyesque lyrics. Then there's 'Bluebird,' a delicate ballad with tasteful choruses and a lovely percussion section. The album was recorded in Lagos, Africa and there has to be a touch of the native influence. 'Mrs. Vandebilt' spans the spectrum of McCartney's songwriting styles. Skipping lightly between the African tribal dance sounds and the majestic chord changes of earlier masterpieces, the band is flawless as is Paul's performance. Denny Laine fills in on Harrison-like guitar solos. This is not reactionary music, it's just damned good music. Lyrically the album is not strong, musically it meets and surpasses everything this kid from Liverpool has ever done before. *Band on the Run* is an album to be amazed at, to tell people about, to buy for your friends and to play constantly."

Rolling Stone's assessment remains memorable. Jon Landau's review seals the record's success and legitimates McCartney's skills as a pop author outside The Beatles:

"*Band on the Run* finds Paul McCartney walking a middle ground between autobiographical songwriting and subtle attempts to mythologise his own experience through the creation of a fantasy world of adventure -- perhaps remotely inspired by his having recently written 'Live and Let Die.' He does it by uniting the myth of the rock star and the outlaw, the original legendary figure on the run.

Up until now, the critical assumption has been that McCartney's lyrics mean little if anything, that he is a mere stylist, playing games with words and sounds. And it is of course possible that the words on *Band on the Run* don't mean (or weren't intended to mean) as much as I think they do. But I'll take a chance and say that *Band on the Run* is an album about the search for freedom and the flight from restrictions on his and Linda's personal happiness. It is about the pursuit of freedom from his past as a Beatle, freedom from the consequences of the drug busts that have kept him from the United States and forced him into thinking of himself as an outlaw (witness the album cover, as well as the title). It is also about two people becoming what they want to be, trying to decide what they want to do, and asking to be accepted for what they are now rather than what they were then.

If the listener were to ignore the music and the skill with which McCartney has developed his theme, the entire enterprise might seem banal. But he holds the record together through the continual intimation that he enjoys the search for freedom more than he might enjoy freedom himself. In the best tradition of outlaw mythology, he makes being on the run sound so damned exciting.

I'm surprised I like *Band on the Run* so much more than McCartney's other solo albums because, superficially, it doesn't seem so different from them. Its superiority derives from a subtle shifting and rearrangement of elements running through all of his post-Beatles' music, a rounding out of ideas that had previously been allowed to stand half-baked, often embarrassingly so. *Band on the Run* is no collection of song fragments (*McCartney, Ram*), nor a collection of mediocre and directionless songs (*Wild Life, Red Rose Speedway*). *Band on the Run* is a carefully composed, intricately designed personal statement that will make it impossible for anyone to classify Paul McCartney as a mere stylist again.

A lesser talent would have taken the escape concept and perhaps woven a simple story around it. But, consistent with his own past, the songs overlap both in their content and sentiments (some are even reprised), the album forming a unit without ever becoming too schematic, literal, overbearing or overtly accessible.

On *Band on the Run*, there are two separate searches going on: McCartney's for himself and the listener's for McCartney. The title song begins soberly, its narrator in jail, his music depressed. Both he and the album explode at the moment of his escape, the new-found exhilaration suggesting that there could have been no such pleasure without the preceding pain and that while

McCartney prefers the former to the latter, he has learned how to cope with both.

From the moment of escape, everything on the album eventually evokes the notion of flight. "Jet," a superb piece of music with an obscure lyric about the McCartneys' dog, suggests an overwhelming desire not only to get away but to get away to someone. It ends up a love song, a tribute to both a person and a state of mind, propelled forward by a grand performance.

In point of fact, *Band on the Run* is closer to the Beatles' style than Ringo, which, though it utilised all the members of the group, is more Richard Perry than Ringo Starr. McCartney's emphasis on amplified acoustic guitars, double-tracked vocals, and a generally thin sound in the middle range, places much of the LP in the *Hard Days' Night*–Beatles VI mould. Despite the presence of pure McCartney elements (the lovely strings, so well done by Tony Visconti, the elaborate percussion so superior to *Ram*'s) references to the Beatles make an important contribution to the album's mythic undercurrents.

But there is no mistaking McCartney's intention on 'Let Me Roll It.' A parody of and tribute to John Lennon's Plastic Ono style, he re-creates it with such precision, inspiration, enthusiasm and good humour that I am hard pressed to remember whether Lennon has recorded even a handful of songs that better it, McCartney goes all the way: a perfect vocal imitation, duplication of the Lennon–Spector production style, use of Lennon's lead guitar punctuations and the simple arrangement (complete with tacky Farfisa organ). 'Let Me Roll It' is McCartney joyfully asserting that he can play his former partner's music as well as Lennon can, at the same time that it stands on its own as a perfectly satisfying piece of work.

'Picasso's Last Words (Drink to Me)' is the album's most personally revealing and one of its most moving songs. Dylan mythologises cowboys; McCartney idealises artists. But his celebration of Picasso's life at the moment of his death quickly turns into a fantasy about his own death. He asks only that his woman sing the same words to him that he sings for Picasso: 'Drink to me, drink to my health, you know I can't drink anymore.' His approach to death is remarkably good humoured and a segue into 'Jet' now suggests an even more grandiose escape than the one from jail.

The album's abrupt and surprising ending suggests that the McCartneys are afraid they may find what they are looking for only to discover that it, too, fails to satisfy them. Thus, they end with only one commitment: to remain a band on the run. That decision has resulted in (with the possible exception of John Lennon's *Plastic Ono Band*) the finest record yet released by any of the four musicians who were once called the Beatles."

From this moment on, McCartney will keep in mind lessons learned from *Band on the Run*. Even though his output will never again reach again the heights achieved by this album, for the rest of the decade McCartney's reputation would appear – from a commercial point of view – to be unassailable.

Notes

1   Lorraine Alterman, *Paul's Grooves Will Grab You*, *The New York Times*, 2 December 1973.

— 11 —
B-SIDES AND OUTTAKES FROM THE SESSIONS

As was mentioned, only one track recorded during the *Band on the Run* sessions remained unreleased at the time. It's "Oriental Nightfish" written by Linda, which will find a place on her posthumous album *Wide Prairie* in 1998. For the B sides of the singles "Helen Wheels" and "Band on the Run" (European version), McCartney dusts off two songs that were previously recorded, "Country Dreamer" and "Zoo Gang".

* * *

Country Dreamer
(Paul and Linda McCartney)

Recording: 26 September 1972 (basic track) and 26 November – 6 December (overdubs) **Location:** Abbey Road Studios, London (basic track) and AIR Studios, London (overdubs) **Release:** B-side single "Helen Wheels" (1973)

The rustic lifestyle led by Paul and Linda in the early Seventies is the background for "Country Dreamer", a pastoral idyll of candid simplicity recorded during the *Red Rose Speedway* sessions but set aside. "We were living away from the city – we were on a farm – and it was great, because both of us had been city dwellers for so long," McCartney says, "but both of us loved nature so the idea of getting out into the country was very attractive. It was good to able to see if we could exist on our own without all the infrastructure of the city around us. It was a huge change in our life."[1]

Paul reveals the inspiration behind it: "I think the first line of 'Country Dreamer' is a nod to Ivor Cutler," he says, "a brilliant Scottish poet and songwriter who once described himself as an 'oblique musical philosopher'. Like me, he was a sucker for the surreal … He wrote a lovely little song called 'I'm Going in a Field'."[2]

Demoed in the summer of 1970 in a version that is practically identical to the definitive one, "Country Dreamer" is an acoustic sketch in a folk vein. The studio recording for the basic track took place 26 September 1972 at Abbey Road with overdubs added at AIR Studios between 26 November and 6 December 1972, and features Paul (vocals, acoustic guitar, and overdubbed piano), Linda (backing vocals), Laine (backing vocals, bass), McCullough (electric guitar) and Seiwell (drums, percussion).

Opening with a guitar arpeggio backed by some percussion effects, the track is well-crafted – although with minor uncorrected imperfections to emphasise its spontaneity (at 0:02 there is a brief off-mike yell and at 0:04 a slip by Laine on bass) – and highlights McCullough's work on pedal steel guitar and McCartney's vocal harmonies. Seiwell's accompaniment relies on brushes. Seiwell: "It's based on leftover feelings from the McCartneys spending time at their farm in Scotland. Paul played acoustic, Denny was on bass and Henry played a pedal steel guitar … Never played one before … Not bad, uh?"[3]

Lyrically, "Country Dreamer" is a gallery of the small daily pleasures of country life, the only experiences that – in McCartney's view – allow one to revisit long-lost sensations and genuine feelings. "My song starts 'I'd like to walk in a field with you/Take my hat and my boot off too'. I like the idea that he's got a hat and boots," Paul says. "In Scotland, it would be raining and muddy a lot, or we'd be on the farm, so you would often have wellies on. They wouldn't be very glamorous boots. But you'd come to a stream, and you'd take them off and get in."[4]

Musicians:
Paul McCartney vocals, backing vocals, acoustic guitar, piano, percussion (?) •
Linda McCartney backing vocals • **Denny Laine** backing vocals, bass • **Henry McCullough** pedal steel guitar • **Denny Seiwell** brushes, percussion (?)

* * *

Zoo Gang

(Paul and Linda McCartney)

Recording: 26 April 1972 (basic track) and 7 May 1973 (overdubs) **Location:** Abbey Road Studios, London **Release:** B-side single "Band on the Run" – UK – (1974)

In June 1972, the legal battle that pitted McCartney against Sir Lew Grade's ATV Music – who disputed the songwriting credits of his songs composed with Linda, since "Another Day" released in February 1971 – reached a settlement.

ATV would accept the joint composing credits in return for Paul agreeing to certain conditions imposed by the company. The first of these had been the TV special *James Paul McCartney*. The second act of the McCartney–Sir Lew Grade saga involved the TV series *Zoo Gang*, based on the adventures of five surviving French Resistance fighters who meet after 20 years, and aired on ATV in six episodes between 5 April and 10 May 1974, Grade asked Paul to write the main theme to it.

McCartney accomplishes his task by delivering this short instrumental, recorded at Abbey Road on 25 April 1973 with Alan Parsons engineering. The lineup consists of only Paul (bass, electric guitar), Linda (Moog) and Denny Seiwell (drums). The track features guitar and synthesizer both characterised by a squeaking tone and has a tribal feel to it. The addition of an accordion (overdubbed on 7 May by Paul himself) adds a French atmosphere to the recording, which can be fully appreciated within the context of the series, set in Nice.

McCartney thought about using the track as the B-side to the single "Band on the Run", planned for release in the UK on 28 June 1974: the TV series would then have ended quite a while before. At that point, Sir Lew decided to move up its release and have others record it. Tony Hiller organised the recording with some session men and with the arrangement of Colin Frechter: that improvised band was called Jungle Juice, and the single was rush released on 24 May 1974 on the Bradley Records label, thus anticipating Wings' version.

Musicians:
Paul McCartney bass, electric guitar, accordion • **Linda McCartney** Moog •
Denny Seiwell drums

* * *

Oriental Nightfish

(Linda McCartney)

Recording: 4 October 1973 **Location:** AIR Studios, London **Release:** *Wide Prairie* (1998)

The only *Band on the Run* outtake, "Oriental Nightfish" is also the only song from these sessions that originates from Africa.

Musically, this is more of a good jam than a real song. Centred on a chord sequence found by Linda on the electric piano, it is an almost entirely instrumental track, except for two spoken interludes: "Linda's dramatic vocal harks back to the Fifties and Sixties when strange stories were told by acts like The Shangri-Las, The Coasters, and others," Paul says.

McCartney contributes bass and drums, also adding an electric guitar part with some stinging solos and riffs, as well and some Mellotron textures, while Laine plays a flute part, heard at the ending, and employed to reinforce the keyboards.

A dramatic track, it goes well with the animated film transposition prepared by Ian Eames sometime later and aired for the first time at the Cannes Festival in May 1978.

Musicians:
Paul McCartney bass, electric guitar, Mellotron, drums • **Linda McCartney** vocals, electric piano, Moog • **Denny Laine** flute

Notes

1   Simon Harper, *RAM* (Deluxe Edition) – *Paul McCartney Archive Collection*, 2012, p. 20.

2   Paul McCartney, *The Lyrics*, 2021, p. 99.

3   Author's interview with Denny Seiwell, 14 November 2011.

4   Paul McCartney, *The Lyrics*, 2021, p. 99.

— 12 —
ALTERNATIVE AND LIVE VERSIONS

*B*and on the Run is among McCartney's most performed albums, over his career he has played eight tracks from the record live. Many alternative versions have also been released over the course of the decades.

*   *   *

Band on the Run

This song was played 731 times between 1975 and 2023. Its live premiere was on 9 September 1975 in Southampton, the first date of the *Wings Over the World Tour*. On the 1979 *Wings' British Tour*, "Band on the Run" was performed with an *a cappella* end section, which involved the whole audience singing the chorus.

Live versions:

[1] *Wings over America* (1976)

[2] *Tripping the Live Fantastic!* (1990)

[3] *Back in the US/Back in the World* (2002–03)

[4] *Good Evening New York City* (2009)

[5] *Live in Glasgow 1979*, download from www.paulmccartney.com (2010)

[6] *Live from Hyde Park 2010*, download from www.paulmccartney.com (2011)

[7] *Live in London 2007*, download – iTunes (2014)

Alternative versions:

"US radio edit", promo single (1974): although never released commercially, this is the version many listeners were familiar with at the time. Lasting 3:50 (instead of 5:08 as in the album version), this edit is shortened by removing various sections throughout the song: the guitar riff at the beginning of the second section is taken out, the orchestral bridge that leads to the third section is shortened and the solo – at 3:52 in the full version – has been removed.

DTS 5.1. Mix (1996): quadraphonic version.

"Nicely Toasted Mix", *Band on the Run – 25th Anniversary Edition* (1999): recorded on 10 December 1998 specifically for this release, this is a short, slowed-down version, which includes only the chorus, with Paul on vocals, acoustic guitar and bass.

"Northern Comic Version", *Band on the Run – 25th Anniversary Edition* (1999): this version was also recorded in anticipation of this anniversary release of the album. Only 00:36 long, it has McCartney on vocals and acoustic guitar: Paul sings in a Northern English accent, in a comical tone, speeding up the rhythm.

"Rehearsal", *Band on the Run – 25th Anniversary Edition* (1999): taken from the rehearsal for the *Paul McCartney World Tour*. Recorded on 21 July 1989 with Paul (vocals, bass), Linda (backing vocals, Moog), Hamish Stuart (backing vocals, electric and acoustic guitar), Robbie McIntosh (electric guitar), Wix (keyboards) and Chris Whitten (drums).

"One Hand Clapping", *Band on the Run – Paul McCartney Archive Collection* (2010): recorded on 27 August 1974 at Abbey Road during the rehearsals that became known as *One Hand Clapping*, from the title of the documentary filmed at the time and left unreleased until 2010. The line-up is: Paul (vocals, bass), Linda (backing vocals, Moog), Denny Laine (backing vocals, electric and acoustic guitar), Jimmy McCulloch (electric guitar) and Geoff Britton (drums).

"Underdubbed Mix", *Band on the Run – 50th Anniversary Edition* (2024): a rough mix prepared on 14 October 1973. It lacks the overdubbing of the orchestra and has the guide vocal rather than the vocal used for the final take for the last part, where electric guitar solos and piano are also missing.

ATMOS Mix, *Band on the Run – 50th Anniversary Edition* (digital only, 2024): Part 1: here we can appreciate more the synthesizer and the vocal harmonies. The separation does a nice job in highlighting the various parts. Part 2: greater clarity on Paul's vocals and guitars. Part 3: The entrance of the orchestra … well if you think the original is powerful, you cannot imagine how it sounds here! Paul's vocal seems to feature a slight reverberation. The accompanying harmonies in the chorus are incredible. Volume of the guitar lick seems to be higher, and they are very well defined. Producer Giles Martin, who worked on the ATMOS Mix of the *Band on the Run* album, has chosen this track as his personal favourite. "I think 'Band on the Run' is like a pop version of 'Paranoid Android' by Radiohead," he says. "The fact it's three completely different songs joined together, but it works as a song. I love that. It's really brave. And I love bravery. It's a pop song that's really brave."[1]

* * *

Jet

The track has been performed live 477 times to date, between 1975 and 2023. "Jet" also made its live debut on 9 September 1975 in Southampton. As a powerful rocker, "Jet" is almost always played during the opening section of the concerts. On the *Summer Tour* 2004 it was the opening number.

Live versions:

[1] *Wings over America* (1976)

[2] *Tripping the Live Fantastic!* (1990)

[3] *Band on the Run* (Deluxe Edition) – *25th Anniversary Edition* (1999)

[4] *Back in the US/Back in the World* (2002/2003)

[5] *iTunes Festival: London* (2007)

[6] *Good Evening New York City* (2009)

Alternative versions:

US radio edit, promo single (1974)

DTS 5.1. Mix (1996): quadraphonic version.

"One Hand Clapping", *Band on the Run – Paul McCartney Archive Collection* (2010): recorded at Abbey Road il 28 August 1974 for *One Hand Clapping*. The line-up is: Paul McCartney (vocals, bass), Linda McCartney (backing vocals, Moog), Denny Laine (backing vocals, electric guitar), Jimmy McCulloch (electric guitar) and Geoff Britton (drums) and Howie Casey (saxophone).

"Underdubbed Mix", *Band on the Run – 50th Anniversary Edition* (2024): a rough mix prepared on 14 October 1973. It lacks the overdubbing of the orchestra, horns and uses the guide vocal. In the ending, we can hear McCartney singing the line later entrusted to the sax.

ATMOS Mix, *Band on the Run – 50th Anniversary Edition* (digital only, 2024): the opening riff seems to balance the horns and guitars better, and the track sounds more aggressive. Great to hear the Moog on the verses more clearly. The lead vocal seems smoother, and the section "Ah Mater" features more strident sounding guitars. The "lyrical" ending is glorious.

* * *

Bluebird

This song was played live 62 times between 1975 and 1976, and again in 2010, when it was back in the setlist for the concert held on 11 November 2010 in Buenos Aires, after being absent for 34 years. As for the two previous tracks, its live premiere was in Southampton, on 9 September 1975. Although "Bluebird" has been not performed live for many years, is often part of the soundchecks, where it has been played 96 times, between 2010 and 2017. Another all-acoustic performance, with Paul and Linda on vocals and performed at CBS-FM radio during a promotional interview for *Band on the Run*, is still unreleased.

Live versions:

[1] *Wings over America* (1976)

[2] *Band on the Run – 25th Anniversary Edition* (1999)

[3] *Wings over America* (Deluxe Edition) – *Paul McCartney Archive Collection* (2013)

Alternative versions:

DTS 5.1. Mix (1996): quadraphonic version.

"One Hand Clapping", *Band on the Run – Paul McCartney Archive Collection* (2010): recorded at Abbey Road on 27 August 1974 for *One Hand Clapping*. The line-up is: Paul (vocals, bass), Linda (backing vocals), Denny Laine (backing vocals, acoustic guitar), Jimmy McCulloch (electric guitar), Geoff Britton (drums) and Howie Casey (saxophone).

"Underdubbed Mix", *Band on the Run – 50th Anniversary Edition* (2024): a rough mix prepared on 14 October 1973. It lacks the overdubbing of the sax solo and features the guide vocal.

ATMOS Mix, *Band on the Run – 50th Anniversary Edition* (digital only, 2024): There are three main features: Paul's vocal, so smooth, the voice blending with Linda in the chorus and Howie Casey's sax solo … we're right there, beside him in the studio.

* * *

Mrs. Vandebilt

Of all the songs of the record, this is the one with the most spectacular live premiere, which happened upon request. McCartney first performed "Mrs. Vandebilt" on 14 June 2008 in Kiev, in a concert to celebrate Ukraine's independence:

300,000 people wildly cheered it. The song had been requested by the Beatles. ru fan club through a petition, that read: "Strange as it may seem, it happened historically that 'Mrs. Vandebilt' was one of most famous and favourite songs of yours among the Soviet people. The 'iron curtain' prevented us from hearing much of the rock'n'roll music. But 'Mrs. Vandebilt' was the song that everybody knew and loved. The lyrics in the refrain 'Ho Hey Ho' could be heard at parties as well as at communist demonstrations, and they were repeated by people of all ages ... Another reason why we are so particular about this song is that the words in the refrain sound very much like the Ukrainian interjection «Гоп» [hop], so the song has a kind of national colouring."

From then on, "Mrs. Vandebilt" stayed in McCartney's setlist up to 2013 and was always met with enthusiasm by the audiences and notched up 120 appearances. From 2016, the track was only presented on soundchecks, with only one further performance, on 25 July 2018, in a special concert at the Liverpool Institute of Performing Arts. An acoustic performance was played by McCartney for the TV documentary *Wingspan*.

Live versions:

[1] *Good Evening New York City* (2009)

Alternative versions:

DTS 5.1. Mix (1996): quadraphonic version.

"Underdubbed Mix", *Band on the Run – 50th Anniversary Edition* (2024): a rough mix prepared on 14 October 1973. Like "Bluebird", it lacks the overdubbing of the sax solo and features the guide vocal.

ATMOS Mix, *Band on the Run – 50th Anniversary Edition* (digital only, 2024): you can really hear the wood of the acoustic guitar. The "Ho Hey Ho" part seems to be higher in volume compared to the original. The electric piano in the bridge and guitars are very well defined. You can hear the slight squeak during the sax solo.

* * *

Let Me Roll It

A real staple of McCartney's live repertoire. Paul always plays electric guitar during the performance, being so proud of its signature riff. Since the concert in Southampton on 9 September 1975 the track has been performed 603 times. Over the 1993 *New World Tour*, "Let Me Roll It" was a spectacular feature, with both McCartney and the guitarist Robbie McIntosh playing on a moving platform above the crowd. Since 2003 the riff of "Foxy Lady", Jimi Hendrix's track, is often played as a coda to the track, giving the opportunity of extending the performance with a jam and some more guitar solos. An acoustic rendition of "Let Me Roll It" was included in the TV documentary *Wingspan* (2001).

Live versions:

[1] *Wings over America* (1976)

[2] *Paul Is Live!* (1993)

[3] *Band on the Run – 25th Anniversary Edition* (1999)

[4] *Back in the US/Back in the World* (2002–03)

[5] *Good Evening New York City* (2009)

[6] *Wings over America* (Deluxe Edition) – *Paul McCartney Archive Collection* (2013)

Alternative versions:

DTS 5.1. Mix (1996): quadraphonic version.

"One Hand Clapping", *Band on the Run – Paul McCartney Archive Collection* (2010): recorded at Abbey Road on 28 August 1974 for *One Hand Clapping*. The line-up is: Paul (vocals, bass), Linda (backing vocals, organ), Denny Laine (backing vocals, electric guitar), Jimmy McCulloch (electric guitar) and Geoff Britton (drums).

"Underdubbed Mix", *Band on the Run – 50th Anniversary Edition* (2024): a rough mix prepared on 14 October 1973. It uses the guide vocal rather than the vocal from the final take. Brief keyboard swirls, later erased, are heard in places.

ATMOS Mix, *Band on the Run – 50th Anniversary Edition* (digital only, 2024): the accompanying guitar at the beginning is so simple and so pure, you can hear the fingers on the fretboard. There is more emphasis on the vocals, and Laine's harmonies stand out. And the big riff is now an even bigger riff.

* * *

Mamunia

Never performed live.

Alternative versions:

DTS 5.1. Mix (1996): quadraphonic version.

"Underdubbed Mix", *Band on the Run – 50th Anniversary Edition* (2024): a rough mix prepared on 14 October 1973. It features the guide vocal.

ATMOS Mix, *Band on the Run – 50th Anniversary Edition* (digital only, 2024): great separation on the harmonies, and the acoustic guitar is very clear. We can appreciate Laine's work on congas even more, especially during the ending. The Moog solo sounds a bit thin compared to the original.

* * *

No Words

A track only played during the 1979 *Wings' British Tour*, for a total of 18 performances, the first on 23 November 1979 at the Royal Court Theatre in Liverpool, the last at the Hammersmith Odeon in London, during the benefit concert for Kampuchea. Live, the arrangement featured a horn section and McCartney's vocal part in the middle was performed with the help of a sound effect (a vocoder or a talking box). Furthermore, the song had a full ending, with an extended guitar solo.

Live versions:

[1] *Live in Glasgow 1979* – download from www.paulmccartney.com (2010)

Alternative versions:

DTS 5.1. Mix (1996): quadraphonic version.

"Underdubbed Mix", *Band on the Run – 50th Anniversary Edition* (2024): a rough mix prepared on 14 October 1973. It lacks the overdubbing of the string quartet and uses the guide vocal. The complete version, lasting 4:33, with a duel between the guitars at the end, is still on the shelf. It was included on a tape auctioned in autumn 2023 by Omega Auctions.

ATMOS Mix, *Band on the Run – 50th Anniversary Edition* (digital only, 2024): great to hear those tight harmonies of Paul and Denny so well balanced and defined. The ending solo has a higher volume.

* * *

Helen Wheels

Never performed live.

Alternative versions:

DTS 5.1. Mix (1996): quadraphonic version.

"Crazed Version"

ATMOS Mix, *Band on the Run – 50th Anniversary Edition* (digital only, 2024): the dirty sound of the tracks seems to stand out even more, the intro in particular being basic and earthy. The harmonies in the chorus put the emphasis on the higher part by Linda. The bass sounds fabulous, especially during the transitions when it's almost on its own. The vocal is definitely clearer, and the guitar licks are loud and clean.

* * *

Picasso's Last Words (Drink to Me)

Only played during the *Wings Over the World Tour* 1975–76 within the acoustic set, in a version shortened to two minutes, the song has racked up 60 performances. The line-up of musicians is: Paul (vocals, backing vocals and 12 string acoustic guitar), Linda (backing vocals), Denny Laine (vocals, backing vocals and 12 string acoustic guitar), Jimmy McCulloch (six string acoustic guitar), Joe English (drums) and Thaddeus Richard (clarinet). In 2001 Paul performed it on acoustic guitar for the TV documentary *Wingspan*.

Live versions:

[1] *Wings over America* (1976)

[2] *Wings over America* (Deluxe Edition) – *Paul McCartney Archive Collection* (2013)

Alternative versions:

"Acoustic version", *Band on the Run – 25th Anniversary Edition* (1999): recorded on 4 December 1998. Another very brief performance on acoustic guitar, prepared especially for the 25th Anniversary Edition of *Band on the Run*.

"Underdubbed Mix", *Band on the Run – 50th Anniversary Edition* (2024): a rough mix prepared on 14 October 1973. It lacks the overdubbing of the strings and woodwind and the vocals from the final take.

ATMOS Mix, *Band on the Run – 50th Anniversary Edition* (digital only, 2024): there is a great emphasis on Linda's high harmony in the verse. During the first "drum machine" segment, we can clearly hear the electric piano. Just near the ending, on the fading, there's a small bass phrase barely that was audible previously.

* * *

Nineteen Hundred and Eighty-Five

The latest addition to the live setlist, chronologically. Played for the first time on 28 March 2010 at the Jobing.com Arena in Phoenix, during the opening date of the *Up and Coming Tour*, "Nineteen Hundred and Eighty-Five" has hardly missed a concert since then, notching up 334 performances. Its fast-moving piano part (with many blues-like sliding notes), combined with the structure of the song and its difficult vocal, made it quite challenging for McCartney, who mixed up the words on rare occasions or made a mistake on the piano. A compelling track, this is one of the most acclaimed by audiences.

Live versions:

[1] Spotify, *Spotify Singles – Under the Staircase* (2018)

Alternative versions:

"Underdubbed Mix", *Band on the Run – 50th Anniversary Edition* (2024): a rough mix prepared on 14 October 1973. It lacks the overdubbing of the orchestra and the vocals.

ATMOS Mix, *Band on the Run – 50th Anniversary Edition* (digital only, 2024): in the intro, piano and electric piano/keyboards have been better balanced in volume, so we can hear them both very well. There is a smoother vocal, and the organ is very present. The piano seems to be more brilliant.

Notes

1   *50 Years On: Paul McCartney & Wings – 'Band On The Run'*,
    Clash, 8 February 2024, https://www.clashmusic.com/
    news/50-years-on-paul-mccartney-wings-band-on-the-run/

— 13 —

COVER VERSIONS: *BAND ON THE RUN* THROUGH OTHER ARTISTS' PERSPECTIVES

A s is the case for all of Paul McCartney's post-Beatles repertoire, the songs of *Band on the Run* have also been reinterpreted by many artists. Here's a gallery of the most significant.

The most covered track is without doubt "Band on the Run" itself, which had at least eight reworkings in 1974 alone. The most notable is by Afro American blues/soul man Richie Havens, who included a version on his album *Mixed Bags II*. His cover squeezes McCartney's track into three minutes: after an instrumental opening of the harmony of the chorus, Havens' remake develops in a highly original manner, alternating the second section ("If we ever get out of here") with the chorus, which this time is sung. The production features the heavy reverbed voice of the singer, backed by slap bass and prominent piano chords. Havens would return to McCartney's repertoire again over the years, covering "Every Night" from *McCartney* (included in *Connections*, 1980) and "Arrow Through Me" from *Back to the Egg*, included in *Simple Things* (1987).

The cover by the Foo Fighters, the band founded by Nirvana's ex-drummer Dave Grohl, released in 2007, also proved very popular. From the point of view of the structure and of the arrangement, it's practically identical to the original, with a quasi-metal-punk slant in the rocking section. It's thanks to this cover that younger generations have discovered "Band on the Run". Grohl and McCartney share a good friendship, and on several occasions the drummer pays a visit to Paul during his concerts, sometimes even duetting with him on this song.

Two former members of Wings have released their own cover of the track: Denny Laine, who in 1996 included it in his collection *Wings at the Sound of Denny Laine*, and Laurence Juber, whose instrumental remake for classical guitar can be found on the album *One Wing* (2005).

Among the covers of "Jet" a real highlight is the one by US rock group Jellyfish, who in 1990 released their version on the UK limited edition of their album *Bellybutton*.

Worth mentioning is the cover of "Bluebird" by singer/songwriter Corinne Bailey Rae, included on the 2014 tribute album *The Art of McCartney*. Bailey Rae's version features a very heartfelt vocal performance and a laid-back accompaniment: it's probably the most accomplished reinterpretation in this project on the music of McCartney.

The folk roots of "Mrs. Vandebilt" make the song perfect for remakes in other languages: for example, the Spanish version by the Los Mismos, with Helen Bianco on lead vocals. The track was released as a single in 1974. Both a fun and enjoyable live performance and another mimed performance aired on the TV program *Señoras y Señores* from TVE can be found on YouTube.

Two versions of "Let Me Roll It" are notable: the first by Robyn Hitchcock, included on the album *Listen to What the Man Said – Popular Artists Pay Tribute to the Music of Paul McCartney* (2001), the second care of Paul Rodgers, and part of *The Art of McCartney* in 2014. Both these covers emphasise the rocking sound of electric guitars, more in line with McCartney's live performances than with the version on *Band on the Run*, which is more bluesy and laid-back.

"Helen Wheels" is a curious case. Its first cover was launched in 1974 in the Finnish language, with the title "Palaa Taas" by an artist (or group) called Jouko Ja Kosti. The effect is quirky. On the other hand, it's a very good remake, both vocally and instrumentally, recreating all the parts with philological precision. More recent is the version by Def Leppard (2014, for the album *The Art of McCartney*, in its Deluxe edition), a heavy metal rendition.

Of wide appeal to the general public is the remix of "Nineteen Hundred and Eighty-Five" by Timo Maas and James Teej released in 2016 with the approval of McCartney.

This 12" single was released on 30 March 2016 on Phonica Record in an edition limited to 300 copies, arousing fans' curiosity. The story is worth telling. In 2009, Maas hears the song in Ibiza, while he's on vacation at the house of his agent David Levy. Maas asks if it's possible to have the multitrack tape and Levy manages to get it. Maas tinkers with the remix over several years, until in 2015 his friend James Teej, a DJ, listens to it and the two start working on it seriously over a weekend.

At that point, Levy gets back in touch with McCartney to provide him the results of the session between Maas and Teej. Paul and his team give their approval to the project. "Once we got into working with the parts, it became very clear what it was we wanted to achieve with it," says Teej. "We worked really hard on re-treating some of the original elements and went for more of a modern style of mixing, specifically heavier and more emphasis on the bass. We also used segments of the full vocal that were not used in the original, but that we felt really reinforced Paul's blues-inspired vocals. I personally believe that

Cover to the 12" single of "Nineteen Hundred and Eighty-Five" by Timo Maas (2016).

this is one of the most amazing vocals Paul has recorded. The main thing I felt was necessary was to have the focus of our version be on Paul's voice, and to use some of the more bluesy elements and emphasise them more. The biggest risk we took was not using the original's iconic main rhythm piano line. By freeing up the space and removing that rhythmic piano structure, it allowed the track to really breathe. The vocal's sheer emotion made this sound like a different record altogether, while still remaining true to much of the structure and core elements of the original. We were very sensitive to not add too many new sounds, however we worked hard to manipulate the samples of all the original amazing parts – oboe, guitar, bass, drums, intro and outro piano and Moog synth – and other melodic elements to really have them all working together. It wasn't the easiest reworking, and we wanted to stabilise the tempo slightly but also have some nods to that progressive style of arrangement found in music of the 60s and 70s. It was a totally organic process overall, and our version was born initially in those three consecutive and intensive days of work. When I returned to my home in Ecuador, I was able to do some of the final touches, as well as work on the radio and club edits which have all now been pressed to vinyl."[1]

Notes

1   Matt Medved, *Mysterious Paul McCartney Release Details Revealed: Exclusive*, *Billboard*, 19 April 2016 https://www.billboard.com/music/music-news/paul-mccartney-mystery-1985-remix-revealed-exclusive-7340722/

— 14 —
BAND ON THE RUN OVER THE DECADES: CRITICAL FORTUNE AND ITS ROLE IN POPULAR CULTURE

I t's no coincidence that *Band on the Run* is the McCartney album that boasts the highest number of releases and reissues. Although it's impossible to keep track of all the various configurations, there are at least nine worth mentioning: the 1975 quadraphonic 8-track cartridge version (prepared by Geoff Emerick and Alan O'Duffy), the first issue on CD in 1985, the 1987 CD (with no bonus tracks), the 1993 CD, remastered by Peter Mew as part of the *Paul McCartney Collection* (this time including "Helen Wheels" as a bonus track for the non US version), the 25th Anniversary Edition (released in 1999 in a mini clamshell box with two CDs, the second containing interviews and some bonus tracks), the 2010 edition – the first issue of the *Paul McCartney Archive Collection*, also available in a Deluxe Edition, which includes a book, 3 CDs and a DVD – and the 50th Anniversary Edition (February 2024, but copyrighted 2023), which contains the album in its US incarnation and a bonus CD with the "underdubbed" versions of nine songs (sort of rough mixes prepared by Geoff Emerick and Pete Swettenham on 14 October 1973, before the orchestral overdubs and the final vocal and instrumental takes were recorded). From the Nineties come both the DTS 5.1. Surround Mix (the CD version of the Quad mix) and the Steve Hoffman Gold DCC remastered edition.

* * *

With a few exceptions, the reputation of the album rode the decades. Many critics and journalists have discussed the album: privileging a philological approach, we have decided not to correct any possible errors – due to incorrect information from those who wrote the following extracts, we report exactly what was written. It's worth starting this overview with a classic, *The Beatles Forever* (1978) by Nicholas Schaffner, the first book of a certain importance that puts the four Beatles' solo careers in perspective, up to that moment.

Schaffner, paving the way for everyone who would assess *Band on the Run* in the future, writes:

"Having decided it might be far out to cut a new Wings album in Lagos, Nigeria, Paul had already made all necessary arrangements when guitarist Henry McCullough and drummer Denny Seiwell announced that he could take that trip without them. Apparently, they felt they were being turned into McCartney-programmed robots and didn't like it any more than George and Ringo had. In their absence, Paul pulled himself together to create an album that picked up where *Abbey Road* left off. In doing so, he combined a sense of urgency with his renewed self-confidence; as Mrs. McCartney told *Sounds*: 'Paul thought, I've got to do it, either I give up and cut my throat or get my magic back.' … While Paul would soon abandon some of the sense of adventure that helped turn *Band on the Run* into as much of a smash with the critics as the public, he would never again forget how to make records."

The same year, there's a very intriguing and meaningful testament to the fact that *Band on the Run* is already grounded in American popular culture. The cover of the *Marvel Treasury Edition*, a special collectors' issue dedicated to Spider Man, shows eight characters that are presented in a very similar way to the *Band on the Run* cover. There is even a wall behind them. The characters are Iron Fist, Angel, Spider-Man, Werewolf by Night, Jean Grey, Iceman, Cyclops and Ghost Rider.

The cover of *Marvel Treasury Edition*, mirroring the original *Band on the Run* shoot.

Of the less generous judgements on the album, an "honourable mention" goes to the well-known and often caustic Robert Cristgau, who in 1981, on his *Record Guide*, portrays it in a more disenchanted way compared to the (sometimes even exaggerated) praise of the previous decade:

"I originally underrated what many consider McCartney's definitive post-Beatles statement, but not as much as its admirers overrate it. Pop masterpiece? This? Sure, it's a relief after the vagaries of *Wild Life* and *Red Rose Speedway* and most of side one passes tunefully enough – 'Let Me Roll It' might be an answer to 'I Want You (She's So Heavy)' and 'Jet' is indeed more 'fun' than 'Uncle Albert/Admiral Halsey'. But beyond those two the high points are the title track, about the oppression of rock musicians by cannabis-crazed bureaucrats, and the Afro-soul intro to 'Mamunia,' appropriated from relatives of the Nigerian children who posed for the inner sleeve with Sah and helpmates."

It is, after all, 1981, and we're in the aftermath of Lennon's death. It's not the best critical moment for McCartney, but *Band on the Run* is the exception when it comes to a career retrospective. In his classic, and often very critical, *The Beatles Apart*, also published in 1981, Bob Woffinden praises the album:

"The song were well arranged, and both the melodies and the lyrics – which explored the themes of flight, pursuit and freedom – were strong. Indeed, there were moments of lyrical excellence. And so, in the twelfth month of the year nineteen hundred and seventy-three, it was proclaimed throughout the world: Paul McCartney is back!"

*   *   *

In 1985, there's an interesting self-tribute to the album by McCartney. At the end of the video for the single "Spies Like Us" – the title track to the film of the same name, starring Chevy Chase and Dan Aykroyd and directed by John Landis – Paul is seen on the famous Abbey Road zebra crossing with the two actors, and they are suddenly caught in a spotlight. A double reference to both the covers of *Abbey Road* and *Band on the Run*. The combination of the album and one of the most enduring myths of The Beatles' history (that of "Paul Is Dead", with all the hints supposedly contained on the cover of *Abbey Road*) is particularly significant.

*   *   *

In 1987, soon after the first wide release of the record on CD, David Prakel in his book *Rock 'n' Roll on Compact Disc. A Critical Guide to the Best Recordings* writes a review of the album, focusing on the technical details of this reissue, at the time the cutting-edge technology of music industry:

"The best McCartney and Wings album. Yet even *Band on the Run* only barely manages to avoid the mawkish and plain bad – the cloying sentiment and out-of-tune harmony vocals on 'Bluebird' take a bit of stomaching when revealed in awesome clarity by CD! Recorded in EMI's studios in London and Lagos, Band has a slightly dated 'flat' complexion to the sound, lacking the glittering digital highs and tight-ass bass of modern recordings. Compact Disc pulls apart the layers of the sound in a slightly unflattering manner. The back-tracked guitar strumming in "Drink to Me" sounds particularly effective and voices and acoustic guitar have a welcome projection. Hiss and a tinny characteristic enrobe 'Nineteen Hundred and Eighty-Five' on the Japanese-sourced review copy."

Another assessment halfway between its technical and musical aspects is by Bill Shapiro on his *Rock & Roll Review: A Guide to Good Rock on CD* (1991):

"Easily, McCartney's most successful and listenable outing, *Band on the Run* was recorded in Nigeria and reflects both his fine pop sensibility and production acumen (most of the sounds that make-up the recording were, in fact, done by McCartney alone in the studio). It does contain some strong Seventies pop product, 'Band on the Run,' 'Jet,' and 'Let Me Roll It' being the highlights. While it goes beyond mere aural wallpaper, it isn't any masterpiece either. The CD's sound, marred by some hiss as well as harshness and distortion, is more open, dynamic, and warm than that of the LP."

* * *

In the mid-Nineties, two rock music guides confirm the relevance of *Band on the Run*. The first is *The All-Music Guide to Rock* (1995), where William Ruhlmann assign four stars to the album and writes:

"On his best post-Beatles album, McCartney uses his mastery of studio technique and gift for musical juxtaposition – from symphonic touches to hard rock to melodic acoustic music – in a wonderful collection of well-constructed songs, including the Top Ten hits 'Helen Wheels,' 'Band on the Run,' and 'Jet.'"

The second is *Musichound Rock: The Essential Album Guide* (1996), with a piece by Roger Catlin, who writes a four-star review of the record:

"Wings' *Band on the Run* was the best conceived, least embarrassing album of Paul McCartney's solo career. With just he, wife Linda and Denny Laine comprising the band, it was recorded in Nigeria, where the rhythms helped give the tunes a sunny disposition."

* * *

In 1999, on the occasion of the release of the 25th Anniversary Edition of the album, a new wave of reviews appear. These are the words of Chris Ingham in *Mojo*:

"In the immediate post-Beatles period, Paul McCartney was a critic's whipping boy. Compared to the lustrous pop of *Abbey Road*, the open-hearted panoply of *All Things Must Pass*, 1970's McCartney sounded shockingly underdone. Those that weren't scornful were perplexed. 1971's *RAM*, while these days sounding rather like a ragged masterpiece, was perceived as more sloppy work from an ex-talent taking this 'loosening up' thing too seriously. His new 'group' Wings, notoriously featuring his missus on elementary organ, debuted with 1971's wilfully shabby *Wild Life* and released peculiar singles like the simple-minded 'Give Ireland Back To The Irish' and the for-the-kids 'Mary Had A Little Lamb'. 1972's *Red Rose Speedway* boasted one bona fide beauty in 'My Love' and almost sounded like a proper record in places, but still fell short of what were by now significantly fallen expectations. Then came *Band on the Run*, and the critical gush that greeted it was the sound of the world sighing with relief that the man who had helped set unmatchable standards for pop music in the '60s wasn't going to spend the rest of his career messing about. Even John Lennon, who had blown raspberries at Macca's earlier efforts, told *Rolling Stone* it was 'a great album … You can call them Wings but it's Paul McCartney music. And it's great stuff.' It is, actually. From the iridescent guitar twang and luxurious ride cymbal groove of the intro to the apocalyptic climax of '1985' – delightfully undermined by an irreverent sing-along reprise of the title track's refrain – *Band on the Run* has a tangible vibe about it. Retaining some of the compelling recklessness of his early solo years but tempered with genuinely inspired artistry, McCartney's customary breezy confidence is, for the most part, entirely matched by the quality of his music. It cooks."

* * *

In 2003, *Band on the Run* is included in the *Zagat Survey Music Guide – 1,000 Top Albums of All Time*. It's a four-star review:

"Paul McCartney proves himself a fab instrumentalist and songwriter with talent that far surpasses his cute Beatles image on this fresh, fun and still listenable disc that flocks of fans feel is the only album that comes close to his legacy with 'the lads.' Recorded under duress in Nigeria, this multi-platinum No. 1 is an unmitigated catchy pleasure thanks to the title hit,

'Helen Wheels' and 'Jet,' chart-topping tunes that make it work incredibly well for parties and long drives."

It's still 2003, when *Rolling Stone* places *Band on the Run* at no. 418 in his special ranking of the best album of all times. This is the accompanying comment by the American magazine:

"Paul McCartney and Wings trekked to EMI's studio in Lagos, Nigeria, for seven stressful weeks to make *Band on the Run*, regarded by many as McCartney's finest post-Beatles hour. Opening strongly with the one-two punch of 'Band on the Run' and 'Jet' (named after Paul's dog), it proved that McCartney still knew how to rock."

In 2004, *Band on the Run* is included in the guide *The 100 Best-Selling Albums of the 70s*, by Hamish Champ. Again, the album is considered the peak of McCartney's discography. Champ writes:

"Paul McCartney's post-Beatles output reached a critical and commercial peak on *Band on the Run*, which brought him to the closest point of reaching the quality threshold of his Fab Four days. His fifth album since quitting The Beatles just three years earlier, this 1973 release avoids the lightweight pitfalls of many of McCartney's solo projects, capturing instead a re-invigorated artist confident again in his abilities.

Mostly created in Lagos, Nigeria, the album's success came despite two members of his band, Wings, quitting on the eve of recording, then Paul and Linda were held at knifepoint in Lagos with their possessions, including the album's demos, being stolen.

The departures left a tight nucleus of the McCartneys and Denny Laine, with Beatles veteran Geoff Emerick engineering and other musicians drafted in where needed. McCartney also called upon a series of famous associates for the front cover shot, including the likes of film star James Coburn and horror actor Christopher Lee dressed as convicts.

Topping both the UK and US chart in the spring of 1974, the album's many highlights include the completely structured title track, a US chart-topper in its own right in June 1974, the powerful 'Jet' and the laid-back 'Let Me Roll It.' 'Helen Wheels,' which reached Number Ten on the singles charts, was inspired by Paul McCartney's nickname for his Land Rover. As of 2004, *Band on the Run* was the #84 best-selling album of the 70s."

Jim Harrington in his guide *1001 Albums You Must Hear Before You Die* (2005) confirms the assessment that *Band on the Run* is McCartney's best work, considering it practically a solo record:

"Paul McCartney's early solo work did little to suggest he could make timeless music outside The Beatles. He delivered solitary gems -- notably 'Maybe I'm Amazed' and 'Live and Let Die' – but full albums such as 1973's *Red Rose Speedway* were not Beatlesque killer. Moreover, McCartney, who had recently garnered headlines for a drugs bust, went to work on this album with more than a few feathers missing – drummer Denny Seiwell and guitarist Henry McCullough split a week before the band flew out to record in Lagos, Nigeria. And when they got there, McCartney and wife Linda were robbed at knifepoint. But out of adversity ... McCartney dominated every inch of what was essentially a solo record. *Band on the Run* kicks off with its rollercoaster of a title track – a kind of mini-suite actually, recalling the heavily nuanced arrangements of the side-two *Abbey Road* song cycle. He immediately makes good on that high-flying start with the punchy 'Jet' and continues to soar through the sunny 'Bluebird.' ... The work momentarily stumbles on 'Let Me Roll It,' a misguided answer to Lennon's scathing 'How Do You Sleep?,' but again finds focus thanks to solid side-two tracks like 'Mamunia' and 'No Words.'

Six (mainly British) celebs co-starred on the prison break cover, half suggesting a scaled down *Sgt. Pepper*. Fittingly so, as *Band on the Run* also proved a critical and commercial hit, and one that stands as the singer/songwriter/bassist's finest post-Beatle hour."

* * *

The fact that *Band on the Run* continues to be part of the American popular culture finds a curious and somewhat impressive proof again in 2005.

The poster for the Dreamworks animated film, *Madagascar*, is a reference to the album cover. In fact, the poster shows the animals, protagonists of the movie – furthermore, centred on their escape from a zoo, a subject linked to that of *Band on the Run* – caught red handed, with a brick wall at their back. All elements that feature in McCartney's album cover: "Actually, marketing came up with that," Tom Grath, co-director of the film laughs. "We saw that, and it seemed funny."[1]

* * *

New celebrations come with the Deluxe Edition in 2010. Here's what's Rob Sheffield writes on *Rolling Stone* on 25 November, with a five-star rating:

"The title track to *Band on the Run* is Paul McCartney's most gangsta moment. Who else could hit Number One with a prison-break epic starring the Jailer Man and Sailor Sam? This remastered three-CD/one-DVD

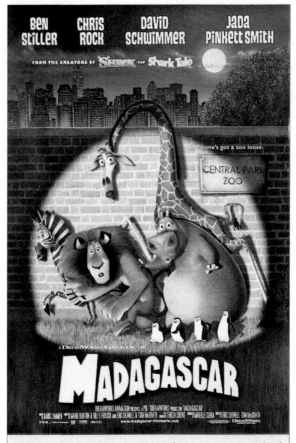

The poster for the animated movie *Madagascar* (2005), a parody of the *Band on the Run* cover.

version of McCartney's best-loved post-Beatles album adds extras like a 120-page book and footage of McCartney recording in Nigeria. But the real action still lies in the original LP's revved-up pleasures: After the sketchy experimentation of his early solo career, which produced highs ('Hi Hi Hi') and low-low-lows ('My Love'), McCartney returned to rocking like he'd never left. 'Let Me Roll It' and 'Helen Wheels' are his shaggiest guitar grooves. 'Jet' is a gloriously daft Bowie takeoff – and Bowie seems to have returned the compliment by turning the spacey New Orleans pastiche 'Nineteen Hundred and Eighty-Five' into 'TVC15.' After *Band on the Run*, nobody ever again claimed Macca couldn't rock."

* * *

The excited reviews in the music press are also confirmed in 2024, for the release of the 50th Anniversary Edition of the album, which also includes the "under-dubbed" versions of nine tracks.

Danny Eccleston in *Mojo* does not stint on his compliments and assigns five stars to the record's new edition:

"Call it The Paradox of Paul. Often thought of as the 'slick one' in The Beatles, closer inspection of his best work often reveals what's charmingly impromptu, even lo-fi. *McCartney I* and *II* are the paradigms, but even on *Band on the Run* – superficially among his most 'crafted' records – there's evidence of a musical mind moving too fast to bother with spit and polish."

Pete Paphides on *Uncut* writes:

"Fifty years on, Macca's miracle continues to define his essence. Context always matters, but in the case of *Band on the Run* – celebrating its 50th birthday with this expanded half-speed remaster and a stripped-back companion version – it's the difference between a great album and a mythical one. Context matters because *Band on the Run* is an album whose essence is inseparable from the superhuman act of determination to which it owes its existence. ...

The 'underdubbed' versions accompanying this reissue reveal that, before arriving at George Martin's AIR studios to finish the job, the Lagos sessions weren't so different to the homespun intimacy of the Wings albums that preceded them. ...

Yet, none of that detracts from the primary energy source of *Band on the Run*. To listen to the album in the wake of Peter Jackson's *Get Back* is to be reminded that this is the same man who, when faced with a group floundering despondently in an alien environment, strapped on his guitar and throttled 'Get Back' out of it before our disbelieving eyes. In the wake of Denny Laine's recent passing, one can only imagine what a bittersweet sensation it must be for McCartney to look at the album's multi-celebrity jailbreak cover and ponder that he and (then British light-heavyweight UK boxing champion) John Conteh are now the sole survivors. And over time, these songs – the bullet points of an entire worldview, no less – will outlive us all. In decades to come, when people wonder what Paul McCartney was actually like, all of the answers can be found on this unassumingly miraculous record."[2]

Notes

1   Julian Phillips, *Escape from Zoo-York: Behind the Scenes of Madagascar*, Skwigly, 25 November 2005, https://www.skwigly.co.uk/behind-the-scenes-of-madagascar/

2   https://www.uncut.co.uk/reviews/ wings-band-on-the-run-underdubbed-mixes-edition-144984/

— EPILOGUE —

What will be the legacy of *Band on the Run* in the years and decades to come? So far, it has had a triumphant run. Fashions and musical tastes obviously change. Nevertheless, timeless work resists such changes.

It's not hard to imagine that nothing could damage the popularity of this record. New generations of fans, for some time, have had a total veneration for Wings and for the Seventies. Paul himself is conscious that he has to nurture this legacy, in addition to that of The Beatles. Since 2010 he's started the mammoth *Paul McCartney Archive Collection* – which nevertheless many fans feel progresses rather too slowly.

Podcast, books, Facebook pages, Instagram profiles and YouTube channels exclusively centred on McCartney's post-Beatles output proliferate all over the world: it's a river in flood that has some of the most beloved moments in *RAM*, *Band on the Run*, *Wings over America* and *Back to the Egg*.

The sense of redemption, the desire of making it at all costs, and the achievement of success as a prize for being able to overcome difficulties are subjects that touch everybody. That's why *Band on the Run* will always be with us.

— BIBLIOGRAPHY —

Badman, Keith, *The Beatles After the Breakup. 1970–2000*, Omnibus Press, 2000.

Badman Keith, *The Beatles. The Dream Is Over – Off the Record 2*, Omnibus Press, 2002.

Baker, Ginger–Baker, Ginette, *Ginger Baker Hellraiser*, John Blake, 2009.

Emerick, Geoff–Massey, Howard, *Here, There and Everywhere. My Life Recording the Music of The Beatles*, Avery, 2006.

Doyle, Tom, *Man on the Run*, Polygon, 2013.

Du Noyer, Paul, *Conversations with McCartney*, Hodder & Stoughton, 2015.

Easter, Mark–Madinger, Chip, *Eight Arms to Hold You. The Solo Beatles Compendium*, 44 1 Productions Inc, 2000 (and "remastered" version from 2020).

Kozinn, Alan–Sinclair, Adrian, *The McCartney Legacy. Volume 1: 1969–73*, Dey Street Books, 2022.

Harvey, Andrew, *Give My Regards to Broad Street,* Pavilion Books, 1984.

Gambaccini, Paul, *Paul McCartney in His Own Words*, Omnibus Press & Schirmer Trade Books, 1976.

Lewisohn, Mark, *Wingspan. Paul McCartney's Band on the Run*, Bulfinch Pr, 2002.

McCartney Paul, *The Lyrics*. Allen Lane, 2021.

McCartney Paul, *The Lyrics* (paperback), Penguin, 2023.

Norman, Philip, *Paul McCartney: The Life* (paperback), W&N, 2017.

Perasi, Luca, *Paul McCartney: Music is Ideas. The Stories Behind the Songs (Vol. 1) 1970-1989*, L.I.L.Y. Publishing, 2023.

Spizer, Bruce, *The Beatles Solo on Apple Records,* 498 Productions, LLC, 2005.

Visconti, Tony, *Bowie, Bolan and The Brooklyn Boy*, HarperCollins, 2007.

Welch, Chris, *Paul McCartney. The Definitive Biography*, Proteus, 1984.

Womack, Kenneth, *Sound Pictures. The Life of Beatles Producer George Martin. The Later Years 1966-2016*, Chicago Review Press, 2018.

Websites

www.paulmccartney.com
www.the-paul-mccartney-project.com

Fanzines

Maccazine, https://www.maccazine.com/

— INDEX OF SONGS —

At Last We Will Be Free ...

— Bluebird

Printed in Great Britain
by Amazon

41967906R00096